101
WHISKIES
TASTE AND ENJOY!

ÖRJAN WESTERLUND

CONTENTS

FOREWORD

Two whiskies a week for a year—is that a big enough allocation to research all the best or most interesting kinds of whisky? No, that's hardly enough with today's overwhelming choice. But it's a start. Sorting out the 101 best whiskies on the whisky market is a challenging assignment. Naturally this will be only a fleeting image of the aromatic amber-colored giant as it rushes by.

In spite of that, the hundred or so whiskies offer the opportunity of presenting an enjoyable collection of both classic gems and inspiring new ones. That is how the whiskies in this book are chosen. There are some that are the nectar of the gods that you really should try before you bring the shutters down. There are also some whiskies that have found a place in the book because they open up vistas, regardless of whether that is due to the fact that they come from Taiwan or the Czech Republic, or simply because they are artisan products made in Colorado!

You can get hold of every kind nowadays, thanks to all the suppliers on the net that offer such a wide range of whiskies. A large number can be obtained from well-assorted liquor stores, and finally there are many that can even be found in food shops with an ordinary assortment.

So—I hope you enjoy your read and that the book will be used and enjoyed. Feel free to use the blank lines for your own thoughts. I also hope that the book will inspire you to discover new whisky finds, so that maybe you can pick up that bottle together with your usual favorite next time you are standing in the shop and choosing!

Cheers, my friends, and good hunting!

The author with a dash of Ardbeg Uigeadail,
on a cool summer's evening in 2014.

SELECTION AND DESCRIPTIONS

Giving scores in a book that just contains favorites and recommendations does not tell you as the reader much about how each whisky came to be in the book. I hope that the descriptions of the nose, palate, and finish will do that.

For a start, the whiskies in the book have mainly been analyzed and assessed without adding water. The descriptions reveal how the character of the whisky changes with water. If nothing is said about it you can assume that the description has been written without water having been added to the whisky.

The selection of the sorts of whisky found in the book has been made to open the eyes and nostrils of the person reading the book, preferably with a glass in their hand. The descriptions may seem unorthodox to the strict wine buff, but they have been written with a love of whisky just as much as with words and terms that you will recognize, everyday scent, and taste associations. Of course I have chosen many words that may be found in more stringent whisky assessments too, such as fruit candies, butter toffee, oak, and peat smoke. But, if I am honest, it is the more unusual ones like marmalade, rubber, gunpowder, glue, and licorice that are fun, especially when they are unexpectedly thrown up in the company of other people at whisky samplings or at home on the sofa with someone you like sampling whisky with.

Finally— do not take it for granted that you will think as I do. Taste and smell are personal things and depend on your mood, so think about it, enjoy or reject my descriptions, and write your own in the space provided. Remember that you know best, only you have your nose!

ABERLOUR A'BUNADH (60.2%)

I REMEMBER that day at the airport, about fifteen years ago, when I saw a mighty bottle on the shelf. A short, fat bottle with a wide neck and waxed cork stood out from the crowd then. It was more conspicuous than a colorful winter jacket in a cold gray street. In its character this whisky is still the same, relatively speaking. Thanks to the strength of the casks and the absence of cold filtering, there is an intensive breath of sherry on all levels. It moves up more than one gear compared with most other modest sherry maturations. A raisin and warm alcohol flavor together also bring out a slight aroma of flowery perfume with hints of ozone. The fruit tone and hint of woodiness are fresher than I remember from the early bottlings. Those tended to have a whiff of maturation in somewhat tired oak casks. Instead, here I find bright flowery, ester-like strength in sherry-colored stretch pants.

THE BODY—fiery in terms of strength, but absolutely quaffable without water. Moderately tinged with the oak cask, albeit with rapidly rising, jammy sweetness offset with alcohol and tannins. With a little water more of the oak and typical sherry notes emerge with a manifest bitterness.

THE FINISH is first dry and slightly bitter, but then comes a flavor that hovers between tutti-frutti and sweet sherry notes. The flavor of strawberry jam develops as the fieriness recedes. Then a certain sweet nuttiness before the whole subsides into an Anton Berg finale with a strawberry center. In a lingering finish the strawberry note remains, coming together and petering out with a very light ferrous taste of dark chocolate. A splendid coffee chaser.

STRENGTH ETC. / SCORE: 1 2 3 4 5

NOSE: ....

PALATE: ....

FINISH: ....

13

AMRUT PEATED INDIAN SINGLE MALT WHISKY
(62.78%)

THE NOSE IS NOT UNLIKE LAPHROAIG, but sweeter and with a broader range. With added water there is a rich oily aroma reminiscent of a mixture of salted almonds and peanuts. There is a slight hint of coconut with a certain sweetness—tarred hemp rope with a chocolate-coated coconut bar in your mouth.

THE PALATE IS CLEAN, but slightly smoky and the whisky has a malty, sweet, and creamy texture. It develops into a more acid fruitiness like a freshly cut red apple wrapped in sauna-smoked ham. With water it is somewhat simpler and tighter, tending toward greater pepperiness.

THE FINISH is first dry with a very smoky peaty tone and a fruity base. It gradually develops into a cleaner, rounder, but oilskin and petrol-like peatiness with some sweetness. The taste of perfumed sherry fruit sweetness emerges toward the end. With water the finish also becomes more astringent and cleaner, and the smokiness does not come through so well—so water this tender beauty with care.

STRENGTH ETC. / SCORE: 1 2 3 4 5

NOSE: ....

PALATE: ....

FINISH: ....

anCnoc

HIGHLAND SINGLE MALT
SCOTCH WHISKY

PRONOUNCED: [*a*-nock]

Light and smooth, complex smoky taste
with a soft note of malt and nuttiness.

Established 1894

DISTILLED, MATURED AND BOTTLED IN SCOTLAND
BY THE KNOCKDHU DISTILLERY COMPANY,
ABERDEENSHIRE, AB54 7LJ.

12 YEARS OLD

anCnoc

HIGHLAND SINGLE MALT
SCOTCH WHISKY

PRONOUNCED: [*a*-nock]

The Knockdhu Distillery nestles under
the black Knock Hill, known to the
locals by its Gaelic name of **anCnoc**.

DISTILLED, MATURED AND BOTTLED IN
SCOTLAND BY THE KNOCKDHU DISTILLERY
COMPANY, ABERDEENSHIRE, AB54 7LJ.

Established 1894

70cle 40% Vol

DL4375

ANCNOC, 12 YEARS OLD (40%)

THE NOSE is very compact and complex. Toffee notes, caramelized almonds, buttery cookies, and vanilla. Granddad's old attic on a warm and sunny day with the smell and dust of the drying wood. A slight whiff of grass.

THE PALATE is first sweet and reminiscent of vanilla creams. Soon fieriness, dryness, and a fresh woody note all develop. Swirl it in the mouth a little and a note of ozone comes through, and then a tight fresh and vegetable note—like rowan berries—that rebounds deliciously in a framework of full and rounded malt syrup sweetness.

THE FINISH is first a plump rounded nougat taste and then develops quickly like a light breath of spirits, a swift handful of ethanol on the taste buds. Then dry and vegetable again. Very rich in tannin, and taut—with a hot creaminess in the background like melting vanilla ice cream with a flavor of hot chili chocolate.

An exceptionally aromatic and flavorsome whisky that is also unusually taut.

From Knockdhu Distillery, or the Black Mountain Distillery as it is often known. A prize-winning whisky too, amongst other things with a gold medal in its class "Best malt whisky 9–12 years old" at the Beer and Whisky Fair in Nacka 2009.

STRENGTH ETC. / SCORE: 1 2 3 4 5

NOSE: ....

PALATE: ....

FINISH: ....

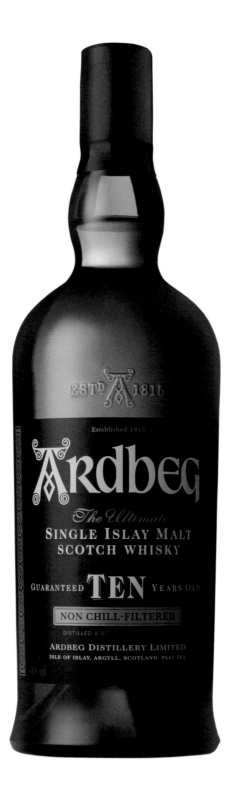

ARDBEG TEN (46%)

THE ATTACK HAS A HINT OF MUSTY PEAT SMOKE ALCOHOL, combined with a whiff of an Asian spice stall, tarred hemp rope, and a slight hint of peppermint. With this a sweet, rounded, and at the same time peaty smoke aroma with hints of salty licorice as if you had just opened a sun-warmed pack of licorice candies.

THE PALATE is full bodied and sweetly grainy. At first young and peppery and then increasingly smoky with a stridently salt licorice maltiness. It develops a sweeter character if you add a few drops of water.

THE FINISH is salty and spicy. Here there are faint notes of salty licorice, some grain husk, and in the longer finish also a hint of cigar smoke and burnt wood.

Matured in bourbon casks.

STRENGTH ETC. / SCORE: 1 2 3 4 5

NOSE: ....

PALATE: ....

FINISH: ....

19

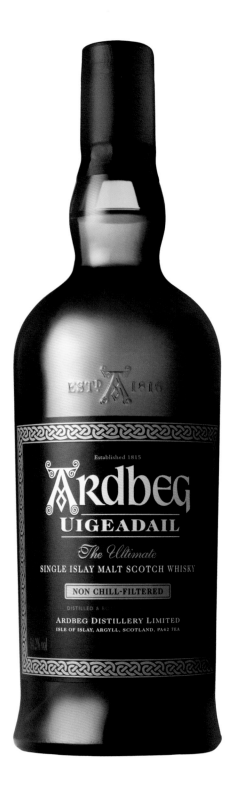

ARDBEG UIGEADAIL (54.2%)

THE NOSE HAS A SLIGHT NOTE OF ROASTED SALTED ALMONDS, WITH SMOKINESS AND FAINT HINTS OF SHERRY. The smokiness is fainter than in its siblings, here more like a cognac with elements of peat smoke. Here too there is the scent of warm fiber board, possibly slightly too much wooden cask, musty brittle toffee from last Christmas—but still a sweet and fruity aroma that is a little reminiscent of dark chocolate.

THE PALATE carries on into more dark chocolate, the chili-flavored variety, with a creamy smokiness and also a touch of salted nuts.

THE FINISH is intense, medium sweet becoming drier. Even more saltiness develops, dry and doughy, and reminiscent of pretzels. A brilliant smoky whisky for all those occasions when you want a softer note in your Islay whisky. Well worth a long and contemplative moment and perhaps a top-up?

Young and old sherry casks.

STRENGTH ETC. / SCORE: 1 2 3 4 5

NOSE: ....

PALATE: ....

FINISH: ....

21

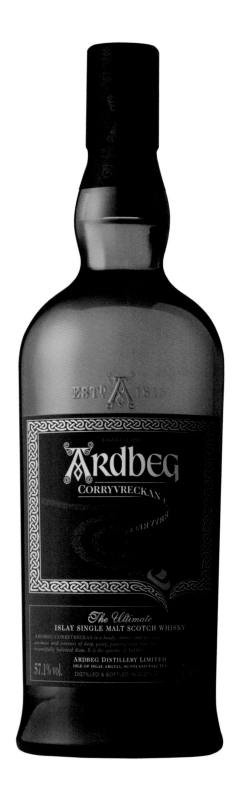

ARDBEG CORRYVRECKAN (57.1%)

A FULL-BODIED AND RICH NOSE that holds much more than just smoke. Here if you sniff you can find aromas of corrugated card, florentines, stuffed cabbage leaves, and apple, and also sweet candy notes such as licorice toffee, strawberry brittle, and the warm heavy scent of pipe tobacco.

THE PALATE IS WELL BALANCED and full bodied, and with a little added water it even acquires a hint of pepper.

THE FINISH carries on into a peppery prelude with a lot of nuances such as mild toffee and chocolate with a strong taste of cocoa. It ends with a bitter cocoa note offset by a sweet smokiness.

First distributed in a short run in 2008, through the Ardbeg Committee fan club, and then to our delight bottled for more public sales since the fall of 2009.

STRENGTH ETC. / SCORE: 1 2 3 4 5

NOSE: ....

PALATE: ....

FINISH: ....

23

ARDBOG (52.1%)

THE JUNE 2013 release from Ardbeg meant a change of name down in the whisky bogs. Every new variety tends to challenge faith in how many times you can create a variation on an already brilliant good smoky whisky. However sometimes it works well, as in this case. The nose is not entirely attractive, having traits of quite musty smoky tones, but also quite a lot of sulfurus nuances reminiscent both of uninflated balloons and sweaty gym mats (the old gray-green ones, barely thick enough to be called mats, like the ones in school gym lessons), and even a faint aroma of soft ripened French cheese. Smoke of course, but wrapped in these powerful associations and with a nugget of hemp rope, seawater soaked with a faint saltiness and clear sweetness in the nose.

THE PALATE is initially creamy smooth and soon turns to both licorice and toffee tones, through a thin veil of tobacco and so on to a faint note of chocolate with raisins. An unusually compact and well-woven smoky whisky, balanced between dominant saltiness, a faint sweetness, and also fruity and creamy components.

THE FINISH is first somewhat like brine-coated sweet licorice. It increases in saltiness and in the longer finish develops a residual taste of faint raisin aromas and a hint of tea.

STRENGTH ETC. / SCORE: 1 2 3 4 5

NOSE: ....

PALATE: ....

FINISH: ....

25

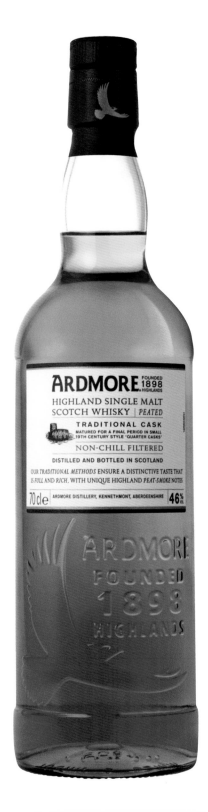

ARDMORE QUARTER CASK (46%)

THE ATTACK HAS THE ACIDITY OF REDCURRANTS AND IS MILDLY PEAT SMOKY. Somewhat rubbery undertone together with the clear sharpness of alcohol. The smokiness has nuances of modeling clay and a hint of fruity heather. There is also a lightness with a few splashes of geranium, fresh mint notes, and bitter oranges.

THE PALATE is peppery with a certain softness and a clear, full-bodied maltiness. The pepperiness increases and so does the fieriness. All this develops almost numbing notes before the sweetness of the malt breaks through and, together with a smoky marmalade tone, calms things down. Also a dry cocoa-like character, with a herby spiciness that reminds me of something as unusual in the world of whisky as parsley!

THE FINISH begins with a sherry-cask smokiness, very like the finish I like in Highland Park. It develops into pretzels and on into a combination of flavors that make me think how delicious it must be if consumed with a room-temperature Taleggio, savory crackers, and a little fig chutney. Perhaps I'm in need of lunch now, but this is a whisky I will happily drink again, either before lunch or with the cheese after dinner. Finely tuned and modulated but nonetheless very powerful.

This peaty Speyside whisky has been matured in the customary way, but differs in that it has been finished for a short time, I guess about six months, in smaller casks—so-called quarter casks—to enhance the cask character of a whisky that is after all quite young.

STRENGTH ETC. / SCORE: 1 2 3 4 5

NOSE: ....

PALATE: ....

FINISH: ....

The Arran Malt

single malt scotch whisky

The Arran Malt Cask Finishes

ISLE OF **Arran** DISTILLERS

EACH CASK
IS SPECIALLY
SELECTED BY
OUR MASTER
DISTILLER

700ml℮

DISTILLED, MATURED AND BOTTLED IN SCOTLAND
ISLE OF ARRAN DISTILLERS LTD, ARRAN
PRODUCT OF SCOTLAND

X1326

CASK FINISHES

The Amarone Cask Finish

The Amarone Cask

The Arran Malt

Single Island Malt
Scotch Whisky

ARRAN AMARONE CASK (50%)

AT FIRST the nose is like that of a fiery red wine, with a full-bodied grape flavor and a splash of cherry and nougat. The nose is dry and rounded rather than marmalade sweet or anything like that. With a teaspoonful of water it becomes milder, more inviting, and fruity, with a note of fresh red apples.

THE PALATE is at first cooling but then quickly peppery and fiery with a mild cask tone. When the aggressive fieriness has slowly subsided, as you swill it in your mouth a balanced, very rounded texture with rugged undertones develops. The whole time there is an echo of a muffled yet rich wine taste.

THE FINISH is straightaway lighter but drawn out into a dry, slightly bitter, and somewhat thin finale. With added water it becomes a little more rounded and sweet, with a faint toffee note, and it actually creeps up a grade.

The age of this whisky is not specified but I would guess about ten years, and one to two years in the Amarone cask.

STRENGTH ETC. / SCORE: 1 2 3 4 5

NOSE: ....

PALATE: ....

FINISH: ....

29

AUCHENTOSHAN THREE WOOD (43%)

FRUIT AND HARD STRAWBERRY CANDIES. Heather flowers and straw-berry mousse. Apples polished with furniture polish, warm wood, and a wonderfully concentrated raisin-like note of dried fruits. A bit like a handful of raisins smell if they are left to simmer gently in butter, whisky, and sugar and plump up again with caramel brown tones. Faint aroma of pecan nuts. Maybe a hint of gunpowder.

THE PALATE is initially like bitter chocolate and develops into a sweeter raisin-like sherry note with a peppery texture on the tongue. The sweet-ness increases and fills the mouth in a particularly pleasing way, in which the body and the sweetness are sufficiently offset by the slightly acrid chocolate note and an elegant, slightly fiery pepperiness, with perhaps a suggestion of waxiness.

THE FINISH is at first short and raisiny and develops into a very well-composed tone of the best sherry-aged whisky. It is balanced and sherry fruity, dry. Neat albeit light. All this soon develops into a grainy character with a bright jam-like and very slightly fiery finale.

In my opinion some of the best that this distillery has released. Triple distilled as usual, with ambitious maturation that after the customary bourbon casks has been completed with both oloroso and Pedro Ximénez casks. The distillery is owned by the Japanese Suntory, in the same group as Glen Garioch and Bowmore.

STRENGTH ETC. / SCORE: 1 2 3 4 5

NOSE: ....

PALATE: ....

FINISH: ....

BALCONES TRUE BLUE 100 PROOF (50.2%)

THIS TEXAS-PRODUCED WHISKY (note the spelling!) has two brothers with more unusual characters: one a luxuriant single malt and the other a smoky rubber tyre article, Brimstone, that even smells like something from the underworld ... well, this corn whisky—that is whisky made from at least 89 percent raw corn and matured in fresh oak casks—is a really successful creation. The nose is a prickly alcohol with a crunchy crème brûlée overtone. It has a strong mix of young spirit and rawness with the burnt dessert-like aromas tacked on.

THE TEXTURE is very rugged and the spirit notes burn the tongue until the whole thing becomes a slightly mineral-like oaky rough tone of cara-melized sugar and corn alcohol. There are also elements of burnt wood in a note that hangs very neatly in the background as a counterbalance to the sweetness.

THE FINISH is spicy and develops into a burnt sweet note that gives a mouth-feel as rough as if you had just eaten fresh rhubarb. The lightly burnt note means that after a couple of minutes there is a feel of well-toasted popcorn left in the mouth. An extremely entertaining whisky experience, an American whisky on laughing gas!

STRENGTH ETC. / SCORE: 1 2 3 4 5

NOSE: ....

PALATE: ....

FINISH: ....

BALVENIE SINGLE BARREL, 15 YEARS OLD (50.4%)

QUITE AN UNDERSTATED NOSE that with a little coaxing and a quest for associations can slowly be connected to the flowery scent of a warm spring with elements of apples and sugar cookies.

THE PALATE is a taut tannin to begin with, but soon enough the smooth fruity taste typical of Balvenie develops, lying on a base of something that could be called a malt-scented taste—rounded and malty and at the same time somewhat ethereal.

THE FINISH sticks to this ethereal malty character that holds both the sweetness and the malt notes for a good while, with faint peaty phenols wafting through at times.

Matured in bourbon casks. Note that the age is the minimum age, at present almost 18 years.

STRENGTH ETC. / SCORE: 1 2 3 4 5

NOSE: ....

PALATE: ....

FINISH: ....

SINGLE MALT ESTD 1892

Distilled at

THE BALVENIE®

Distillery, Banffshire

SCOTLAND

PortWood®

EXTRA MATURED IN PORT CASKS

AGED **21** YEARS

*From our rare reserves of 21 year old Balvenie,
our Malt Master has selected only that whisky which
he believes will acquire even greater complexity and
depth of flavour from further maturation in Port Casks.*

MALT SCOTCH WHISKY

THE BALVENIE DISTILLERY COMPANY, BALVENIE MALTINGS,
DUFFTOWN BANFFSHIRE, SCOTLAND AB55 4BB
PRODUCT OF SCOTLAND

700ml   40%vol 40%alc/vol

The Balvenie single malt scotch Whisky was first distilled on the 1st of May 1893

Distilled, Dufftown, Banffshire

BALVENIE PORT WOOD, 21 YEARS OLD (40%)

JUICILY FRUITY, SLIGHTLY ACIDIC NOSE with the typical Balvenie malty perfume note in the background. A little of the sweetness of berry fruits and a little of newly baked sponge cake also come through.

THE PALATE is buttery and berry-like, and has traces of shortbread with intense malty tones and elements of dark marmalade. Delicious!

THE FINISH is intricately jam-like, malty and taut without being dry. It is reminiscent of the feeling in your mouth after you have thirstily downed a glass of fairly weak unsweetened fruit juice made from strawberries, blackcurrants, and a few cherries. Long into the fading echoes of the taste a little peat smoke also develops. An excellent matured whisky that holds its own well, perhaps with a piece of fruit chocolate or a creamy cigar.

Bourbon cask and finishing for 6–9 months in port pipes.

STRENGTH ETC. / SCORE: 1 2 3 4 5

NOSE: ....

PALATE: ....

FINISH: ....

37

AGED 12 YEARS
THIS RICH, AROMATIC SINGLE MALT
FROM JEREZ.
MATURED IN
SHERRY WOOD
ESTABLISHED 1898
THE
BenRiach
SINGLE MALT
SCOTCH WHISKY
12 YEARS

BENRIACH, 12 YEARS OLD (46%)

FRESH, bright, and succulently raisin-accented nose that has a certain acidity and even conjures up peat smoke, as well as soft toffee and orange brittle. Very promising characteristics in a coffee chaser!

THE PALATE is initially a bite of chocolate and then a malty rounded and slightly peppery note of acidic strawberry jam, soon overtaken by chocolate flakes.

ONLY IN THE FINISH is there a very rich fruity sherry note, plump juicy raisins, and a slightly more strident oak, a whiff of peat smoke, and a faint vegetable tone, perhaps a little reminiscent of dill.

STRENGTH ETC. / SCORE: 1 2 3 4 5

NOSE: ....

PALATE: ....

FINISH: ....

BENROMACH ORGANIC (43%)

OAKWOOD, SWEET ROWANBERRY JELLY, AND DRY BOURBON— along with coconut and resinous oakwood. Vanilla and burnt varnished wood. Powerful but not intrusive or in any way vulgar. Just strong.

THE PALATE IS DRY WITH A CARAMEL-SWEET MALT in the background. A cask tone that feels like a blend of a rounded, sweet Shiraz wine a few years old vying for attention with a malty and at the same time bourbon-like whisky character. The sweetness increases and so does the mildly roasted oak tone. The whole develops into an oaky Irish but harsher whisky, yet without a hint of cats.

THE FINISH IS AT FIRST MILD, with burnt oak in a spicy form like an extremely dry mulled wine with cloves, a little allspice, and a few raisins. Later in the finish cinnamon and something that feels like a dry, nutty, vanilla tone with warm malt and seed husks in the finale.

The Benromach distillery was bought by the independent bottler Gordon & MacPhail and started up in 1998. This organic whisky is matured in casks made of fresh American oak. The reason for this is that it is impossible to get hold of guaranteed organically treated sherry or bourbon casks. The casks are made as hogsheads and burned inside before the raw alcohol is poured in. Benromach Organic was launched in April 2006.

—The result is a whisky that is fruity, viscous, and surprisingly dark, even for the manufacturers themselves, according to Neil Urquhart of the Gordon & MacPhail's owners' family.

STRENGTH ETC. / SCORE: 1 2 3 4 5

NOSE: ....

PALATE: ....

FINISH: ....

41

BERNHEIM ORIGINAL STRAIGHT WHEAT WHISKEY (45%)

THE NOSE is very much like a bourbon, but this whiskey has a lighter character. Here you find a musty, dry, mineral note and also nuances of vanilla toffee and caramelized sugar. All with the difference that the overall impression is more delicate and light on its feet compared with a plump bourbon filled with fruit flavors, coconut, and toffee. The wheat provides a faint aroma reminiscent of wheat dough.

THE PALATE is soft and slightly fiery. As in the nose, everything is very well integrated. The wheat gives a leaner taste than corn. The whole has a delicious dryness, a medium body, and a typical American oak tone.

AT FIRST THE FINISH has a very short, clean, burnt woody note. Then a fruity nuance emerges, a whiff of fruit. Then there is a grainy tone that reminds you more of the taste in the mouth when you have eaten some uncooked dough than of the customary seed husk flavor. The upshot is that this rare whiskey, made of more than 51 percent raw wheat, displays a nose and a palate that make it the Alsace Riesling of the American whiskey world; dry, taut, and mineral-like. It is an interesting alternative both for first impressions and for anyone who thinks there can be too much of the plump candy tones in more corn-rich American whiskeys.

STRENGTH ETC. / SCORE: 1 2 3 4 5

NOSE: ....

PALATE: ....

FINISH: ....

BIG PEAT (46%)

THERE IS SOMETHING OF THE FEEL OF THE SWEDISH MOVIE *HUGO AND JOSEPHINE* when you look at this label. The person who dreamt up the idea of the cartoon sea dog must have thought it was worth standing out and being really original rather than being attacked for trying to look like one of the established peat models.

THE FIRST THING THAT STRIKES ME ABOUT THIS WHISKY—apart from the label!—is that its oiliness comes through even in the nose. Of the many peat-smoked whiskies that have been reviewed, this is one of the more oily. It has a youthful charm, at least for me, as I like stubborn young Islay whiskies. Here there are aromas of oil-based pastel crayons, a hint of rubber mats, and a sweet and sour hint of Crema di Balsamico.

THE PALATE is first peppery sweet and plump, as befits a young whisky of this type. My spontaneous reaction is that there is a lot of Ardbeg in this. The body becomes even more full when it is swilled a little. Here there is an intense saltiness that, with the smoky tones, becomes a little sharp, just as the saltiness in some licorice is sharp.

THE FINISH is waxily oily, like an oil-based crayon or the smell of graphite grease. After the gasoline notes have faded a characteristic sweet note together with peaty notes develops and it tastes like the smell of a piece of wet tarred hemp rope. A real knockout that, for anyone who likes oily young Islay, is a real find. The rest of you will presumably turn your noses up …

STRENGTH ETC. / SCORE: 1 2 3 4 5

NOSE: ....

PALATE: ....

FINISH: ....

45

BLANTON'S STRAIGHT FROM THE BARREL (65.3%)

THE NOSE IS warmly welcoming and cosy. There are soft woody tones like a sun-warmed cigar box or a newly heated dry sauna. A certain sharpness and acidity is there too, similar to a newly chewed lead pencil. On top of that a lovely combination of vigorous burnt sugar sweetness and vanilla develops, like the well-cooked edges of a cake. The whole nose hovers between the bitter brittle and vanilla smooth aroma of cream toffee. With added water the nose becomes mild. The caramel sweetness acquires a top note of pear and the nose moves on toward honey and grain.

THE PALATE is razor sharp without water. In spite of that there is a wonderful note of arrack, overripe banana, and caramelized sugar. It is full bodied and in the first sip very like a good dark rum, albeit with elements of nail varnish, but this soon turns into a clearly oakier and more expected bourbon note. With added water the taste becomes more rugged. Watering it produces more of fresh oak and a little beeswax.

A WARMING AND MEDIUM SWEET FINISH with caramel notes. A light, rugged oak note and toward the end a touch of grain.

One of the very best American whiskeys. Far more finesse than the bottle suggests, with its shape between a hand grenade and a lampstand. With its color a shade of Coca-Cola, you can see that hard-burnt casks and many years in the warehouse have laid the foundations for this whiskey, particularly as Americans do not color their whiskey. On the hind hoof of the galloping horse on the label is a letter—get started and collect all eight!

STRENGTH ETC. / SCORE: 1 2 3 4 5

NOSE: ....

PALATE: ....

FINISH: ....

BOOKER'S BOURBON, 6 YEARS OLD (63.35%)

THE SMELL OF ALCOHOL PRICKS THE NOSE so that it feels like pins and needles. Something of all-purpose household glue. Glue meets newly harvested corn and freshly cut oak. This grandiose full-strength bourbon smells like a bite right through a coconut candy—coconut on top, then the chocolate, the gooey filling, and finally the wafer. A little turpentine-weighted oak wood works well with a succulent juicy freshness.

THE PALATE is rounded and fiery. The sweet bourbon corn notes are softened and develop to create a fine balance between oak and sweetness.

THE FINISH is straightaway a very rich coconut and fruit. There are vanilla-soft oak notes and the wood produces a warm dryness on the tongue like a Luna bar or a Bounty bar swallowed ten minutes before and washed down with a really good bourbon …

Manufactured by Jim Beam. A rarity partly because of the brilliant move in letting the legendary Booker Noe, former head of production at Jim Beam, choose his favorite casks that are sold under the name of this brand in bottles with the original strength of the cask. It is good to drink Booker's on a warm evening, when the sunlight is bathing the walls in evening light. Savor it like iced tea—with ice and water—and discover how the strength and flavor provide a fantastic crispy character in an almost unbeatable long drink. Yeee-ha!

STRENGTH ETC. / SCORE: 1 2 3 4 5

NOSE: ....

PALATE: ....

FINISH: ....

49

BOWMORE LAIMRIG, 15 YEARS OLD (54.4%)

IMAGINE how surprised and happy I was to see this on the shelf! The cylindrical box was in the cart in no time. Sometimes I find the mixed aroma of lavender and fabric sticking plasters that surrounds Bowmore somewhat hard to take, but with that absent this one scores full marks.

THE NOSE is more redolent of sherry and alcohol than any peaty Islay character. For anyone who has had the privilege of fishing sherried whisky from a cask in the cool of the warehouse this is a familiar scent. When water is added the alcohol fumes become muffled, which encourages the fruity and slightly peaty character. Above all it calls to mind those hard, crunchy English fruit candies. Maybe they are chewed in front of a coal fire, sitting in a gaudily upholstered flowery armchair.

THE PALATE is initially a really creamy sherry-like marmalade. It develops into a bite of fire on the tongue. But I swill my way through the flames to land on a soft oaky bed of the best sherry notes. These are sandy and musty but nonetheless deliciously raisin-fruity and tinged with a little phenolic peat smoke. Fifteen years is absolutely perfect here. More would be too much sherry and less would risk letting the sticking plasters loose.

THE FINISH is mildly warming and has a lot of a dark, oxidized marma-lade. There is a pleasant dryness, thanks to the fifteen years, and the tannins gradually tend to grow. The whole time there is a backbone of dried fruit that increasingly clearly develops precisely into the sherry taste. This whisky makes me think of Islay. That hits the jackpot, don't you think?

STRENGTH ETC. / SCORE: 1 2 3 4 5

NOSE: ....

PALATE: ....

FINISH: ....

BULLEIT BOURBON (40%)

MY IMPRESSION OF THE NOSE is of a rounded and well-polished car—a well-made little Japanese one that is reticent in attitude. Butter toffee attractively wrapped in oak. A slightly burnt caramel note from the cask is offset by a light spirit note, on the whole attractive, composed, and relatively light in character. In the recipe, the whiskey's mash bill, the maize had to take a back seat since this bourbon contains about 28 percent rye, twice as much as the usual 15 percent or so.

THE PALATE is at first somewhat fiery and with a light but clear note of butter toffee. The fieriness increases but peaks and then recedes. It is fruity with vanilla brittle notes like jelly beans with an element of raspberry. The cask character comes toward the end.

THE FINISH is at first cask accented and spontaneously has all the traits and butteriness of bourbon. Something of a sweet loaf of bread also makes itself felt. Very much a bourbon to start your habituation with if you have not developed a taste for this drink. Bulleit is good, uncomplicated, and works in any warm weather. So, if you are uncertain about bourbon get stuck into this one! If you then fancy a more unruly character to develop with, move on to a Blanton's, for example.

Bulleit? Well, admittedly it's rather like the name of an immortal movie character played by Steve McQueen. But in this case it is the name of a family that has produced whiskey since the 1830s. Today Bulleit is a revived trademark with a high content of rye and a medium maturation time of about six years.

STRENGTH ETC. / SCORE: 1 2 3 4 5

NOSE: ....

PALATE: ....

FINISH: ....

53

ESTD 1881

AGED **12** **YEARS**

Bunnahabhain™
ISLAY SINGLE MALT SCOTCH WHISKY

XII

NATURAL COLOUR UN-CHILLFILTERED
DISTILLED, MATURED & BOTTLED IN SCOTLAND
The Bunnahabhain Distillery Company
Bunnahabhain, Isle of Islay, Scotland.

70cl ℮   PRODUCT OF SCOTLAND   46.3%vol

F228484

F228485

BUNNAHABHAIN, 12 YEARS OLD (46.3%)

A VIGOROUS, FRUITY NOSE with brisk, warming, alcohol notes against a background of faint but distinct peat smoke. There is a feeling of creaminess here, and with that the often familiar aroma of freshly crushed blueberries. With a few drops of water the sherry notes become clearer, together with a briny note from the phenols.

THE PALATE is initially darkly malty like Weetabix. A rich creamy note soon emerges beneath it. The heat from the alcohol is palpable in the middle of the tongue and the grainy notes roll round in this fieriness that soon also acquires an aroma of burnt wood and a hint of ozone.

THE FINISH is also grain accented and then develops into a rather rugged but warm and crackly final burst, with tones of slightly burnt caramelized hazelnuts.

STRENGTH ETC. / SCORE: 1 2 3 4 5

NOSE: ....

PALATE: ....

FINISH: ....

Bunnahabhain™
ISLAY SINGLE MALT SCOTCH WHISKY
CRUACH-MHÒNA
Since 1881

| Batch | no. 6 | Master Distiller | |

NATURAL COLOUR UN-CHILLFILTERED
DISTILLED, MATURED & BOTTLED IN SCOTLAND
The Bunnahabhain Distillery Company
Bunnahabhain, Isle of Islay, Scotland.
1 Litre ℮ PRODUCT OF SCOTLAND 50%vol

BUNNAHABHAIN CRUCH-MHÒNA (50%)

YOUNG, FIERY, SPICY, AND WARMING and with an element of licorice and a dash of saffron, a phenolic note like an oilskin jacket, and all of this with a hint of a naval, perhaps bladderwrack-scented, overtone.

THE PALATE is at first peanut flavored and salty, tending toward a fiery and still nutty character. The sweetness comes through strongly, like cotton candy on pretzels.

THE FINISH has a young peaty character and yet a good balance between sweetness and a taste that makes me associate it with modeling clay and marzipan at one and the same time, while I also get a feeling of creaminess, as if I had just swallowed a creamy milk chocolate truffle.

Cruach-Mhòna is the name of the stacks of peat that the newly cut turf is piled in to dry out over the summer. The name of the distillery, Bunnahabhain, means "estuary." This Islay distillery quite frequently makes special bottlings like this, often with younger and markedly peat-flavored content, with no color- ants, and without cold-filtering.

STRENGTH ETC. / SCORE: 1 2 3 4 5

NOSE: ....

PALATE: ....

FINISH: ....

CAOL ILA™

MOCH™

ISLAY SINGLE MALT SCOTCH WHISKY

Soft, smooth, clean and fresh, CAOL ILA MOCH (in Gaelic, 'dawn')
evokes the dawn of a new day, slowly prising Caol Ila from its slumbers
and picking out the shoreline of its little wooded bay.

Caol Ila Distillery, Port Askaig, Isle of Islay.
Caol Ila distillery lies close to Loch nam Ban, source of its pure mash water. Appreciated for its
smooth, fresh style, it is lighter-bodied than many Islay malts. Fresh and clean, CAOL ILA
MOCH is an essential expression of this unmistakable, smooth and peaty Islay character.

CAOL ILA MOCH (43%)

"MOCH" is said "to mean "dawn" in Gaelic. Like a spring morning outside the distillery perhaps. The nose has a fresh note of sea air with a breath of lilac blossom. In addition to that there is a clear aroma of licorice chewing gum with a pinch of peppermint. All well applied, like the cream on a well-made gateau, and beautifully formed on top of a thin base of sun-warmed roofing felt.

THE PALATE is first fiery and drily ozonized. With a little sipping the bourbon cask's contribution of vanilla comes through like a flash of milk chocolate. Soon after the whole touches bottom in a taste of fruity multi-flavored licorice.

THE FINISH has a peppery prelude that wafts along toward salted roasted almonds and ends in grain and licorice, sharply salty like the delicious powder you sometimes get on licorice almonds. Childishly delicious with a dry finale.

This is admittedly young and unpolished but it is not without finesse. To an Islay lover I would be so bold as to say that this is one you just have to try. On a rainy early summer's day it is irresistible before dinner!

So far this is the youngest independent tapping from Caol Ila. According to information from Diageo, it is about eight years old and it is clearly up to the weight of Ardbeg Ten and Octomore, for example.

STRENGTH ETC. / SCORE: 1 2 3 4 5

NOSE: ....

PALATE: ....

FINISH: ....

59

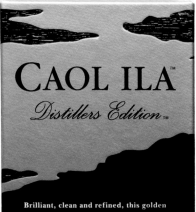

CAOL ILA

Distillers Edition ™

Brilliant, clean and refined, this golden
CAOL ILA DISTILLERS EDITION
has a deep, sweet and smoky flavour
profile that suggests the intense,
saturated colours of late afternoon
sunshine after a storm has passed.

Caol Ila Distillery, Port Askaig, Isle of Islay.

43% vol

SPECIAL RELEASE

C - si; 8-472

LIMITED EDITION

Distilled in 2000, Bottled in 2012

ISLAY
SINGLE MALT SCOTCH WHISKY

THE
Distillers Edition ™

CAOL ILA™

ISLAY SINGLE MALT SCOTCH WHISKY

SPECIAL RELEASE

C-si; 8-472

LIMITED EDITION

DOUBLE MATURED IN MOSCATEL CASK WOOD
BOTTLED IN 2012, DISTILLED IN 2000

Caol Ila Distillery, Port Askaig, Isle of Islay.

CAOL ILA DISTILLERS EDITION, MOSCATEL (43%)

LIKE SITTING EATING FRUIT CAKE beside a peat-fired oven. There are hints of sweet, dried fruit—apricots and raisins with a malty sweetness—and a noticeable smoky tone. And a hint of modeling clay!

THE PALATE is fantastically smooth and faintly sweet and rounded. It develops into an increasingly biting fiery tone with growing peat smoki-ness that then calms down a little and sails on in a balance between well-judged sweetness and smokiness. This is a whisky I don't want just to swallow but to carry on indulging in.

THE FINISH is first smoky with a note of rum and raisins and a little nutti-ness. The smokiness remains while the fruity notes recede and it develops into more of a sweet licorice root. This vintage is an exceptional refinement of an already very good whisky.

Distilled in 1998 and bottled in 2011. The muscatel grape, together with the Pedro Ximénez, is one of the commonest grapes in the manufacture of sweeter sherries and Montilla. The bottle code is "C-si; 8-472."

STRENGTH ETC. / SCORE: 1 2 3 4 5

NOSE: ....

PALATE: ....

FINISH: ....

Colorado
Straight Bourbon
Batch № 39   Bottle № 863   *Whiskey*

500ML ALK. 46% VOL {92 PROOF}

COLORADO STRAIGHT BOURBON (46%)

THE NOSE is light and flowery, with almost perfume-like elements. The youthfulness of this whiskey teeters on the brink of coming through but the presence of excessively unmatured traits is only marginal.

THE PALATE is at first sugar sweet and rapidly develops into fiery, even though the sweetness remains and raises the quality as it increases in both fullness and fruitiness. Fortunately the alcohol keeps the reins short and the lead firm so that the fruit and floweriness cannot get carried away and bolt.

THE FINISH is, to say the least, vigorous and aromatic, but it too keeps on the right track even if notes of rose and Turkish delight waft past. Young, attractive, and unusually a hint of heavy, suffocating, sweet brûlée traits. Young, smart, and elegant like a youthful Frank Sinatra in a tailored suit and narrow black tie.

The Peach Street Distillers in Palisade, Colorado, work in the traditional old way with whiskey, just as they did when they founded the highly thought of Ska Brewing Company. This brewery is rated amongst other things for its Modus Hoperandi, a well-made real ale with generous measures of hops.

STRENGTH ETC. / SCORE: 1 2 3 4 5

NOSE: ....

PALATE: ....

FINISH: ....

63

DALMORE MATUSALEM FINESSE, 15 YEARS OLD (56.7%)

THE NOSE is warm and snug. Seared, berry-like notes, prunes, and a harmonious aroma that combines brittle toffee, nuts, and strawberry candies in a fragrant atmosphere that can only be matched by a book-scented oak-paneled drawing room with leather armchairs. The room is probably imbued with the scent from an open decanter of heavily sweet and nutty PX-sherry—with a few glasses for us. This is my next Christmas whisky. A few drops of water also call forth a faint phenolic note.

THE PALATE is smooth and like a chocolate dessert. Unwatered it is of course hot, but it develops more grape and rugged cask notes, here too with a rich spiciness and something of a hazelnut note. The sweetness increases with added water.

THE FINISH is marzipan and hard orange toffee. It begins stiffly like an elderly lieutenant colonel, but soon becomes sweetly fruity like citrus marmalade or a stiff granny with thick gray hair stirring a pan of fruit. In the longer finish, toward the end there is a faintly sweet orange toffee note that would cause any whisky lover to smile.

One of three releases with different subtitles according to the type of sherry previously stored in the casks—Amoroso Finesse, Apostoles Finesse, and this one. The names give away something of the whisky's character to a sherry devotee. There is an explanation for anyone obliged to choose between them. Words mentioned for all three are orange marmalade, citrus and clove, honey pears, apricot, marzipan, and ginger.

STRENGTH ETC. / SCORE: 1 2 3 4 5

NOSE: ....

PALATE: ....

FINISH: ....

THE FAMOUS GROUSE PORT WOOD
CASK FINISH (40%)

FIRST A HINT OF THE SPICY AROMA of green apples that is then trumped by fresh figs. In the background a slightly musty balancing but not disruptive note, that with a few drops of water can be freshened up and developed into a very discreet scent of peat.

THE BODY is very smooth to begin with, and with an increasing and very clear malty flavor that is filled with fruity sweetness. The fieriness is weaker than that of the standard Grouse but it is there.

THE FINISH is a direct note of peat and continues into a mixture of fruit with a few raisins and a little milk chocolate that fades into a moderately long, warm and astringent seed taste.

The maturation of this far too common variant of the Famous Grouse has gone from six months to three in port casks but fortunately in better casks. I don't mind that, it is a price worth paying!

STRENGTH ETC. / SCORE: 1 2 3 4 5

NOSE: ....

PALATE: ....

FINISH: ....

67

Four Roses

SMALL BATCH

tucky Straight Bourbon Whiskey
ted from Four Select Bourbons

% vol   70cl ℮

FOUR ROSES SMALL BATCH (45%)

THE NOSE is somewhat surprising in its timid emergence—light, acidic, and freshly oaky. There is an element of brisk aromas that goes well with the robust, heavily sweet bourbon character. The fumes spread fruit notes of wine gums, toasted oak wood, and a little raspberry toffee.

THE PALATE is coolly creamy, like a piped soft toffee sauce. An astringent alcohol note with something of a rye character expands noticeably. In the background it brings with it a fruit candy note like raspberry shoelaces and fruit jellies.

THE FINISH is pure burnt oak wood and admittedly it is simple, in the sense of uncomplicated, but there is no lack of richness. There is everything in the palate that can be expected of a bourbon: vanilla, oak, candied sugar, jelly beans, and coconut.

STRENGTH ETC. / SCORE: 1 2 3 4 5

NOSE: ....

PALATE: ....

FINISH: ....

AGED
[12]
YEARS

OLDMELDRUM ABERDEENSHIRE
SCOTLAND

Glen GARIOCH

HIGHLAND | Single Malt Scotch Whisky

Hand crafted since 1797, this NON CHILL-FILTERED 12 year old single malt gains its distinctive Highland character from a classic marriage of BOURBON & SHERRY CASKS. Fresh heather, poached pears and just a HINT OF OAK.

AGED TWELVE YEARS

Non Chill Filtered

N & A Manson

TASTING NOTES: FRESH HEATHER, PEARS AND THE SWEETEST OF CRÈME BRULEE, SWEET RIPE A HINT OF OAK GIVE THIS AND MEMORABLE FINISH

GLEN GARIOCH, 12 YEARS OLD (48%)

THIS WHISKY has a distinctive and very clear fruit aroma. It is hard not to think of coffee, chocolate, and perhaps cigars since the nose of this whisky rapidly dances round like sunbeams in the room it has just been poured in. The strange thing is that in spite of its rich fruitiness, the nose is heavy, it has hints of the smell you notice when you stick your nose in a bag of mixed dried fruit. There is a chocolate-like note that, together with the fruit, makes me want some richly creamy milk chocolate, mixed with a little nougat and rum and raisin. And then a tempting, faintly phenolic edge that embellishes the whole.

THE PALATE is lighter than expected and has a more bracing fiery note than the nose might lead you to suppose. However, the fruitiness is clearly there and fully balances the raisin notes and an increasingly candied fruit-tinged malty sweetness, completely intertwined with a thin streak of smoke.

THE FINISH is at first reminiscent of fruit candies and at the same time dry and malty with a taut bitterness and a slight smoky note. It may seem almost too thin considering the flamboyant nose. The tautness in the finish is like heather-scented schnapps, and on closer consideration this is needed to keep this very generously fruity whisky out of the loath-some ditch it could have fallen into if the candy taste and sweetness had upset the applecart. Instead, as it is now, it is a nice and reliably consistent whisky, well balanced, with the fruit still in the basket and a streak of smoke in the slipstream afterward.

STRENGTH ETC. / SCORE: 1 2 3 4 5

NOSE: ....

PALATE: ....

FINISH: ....

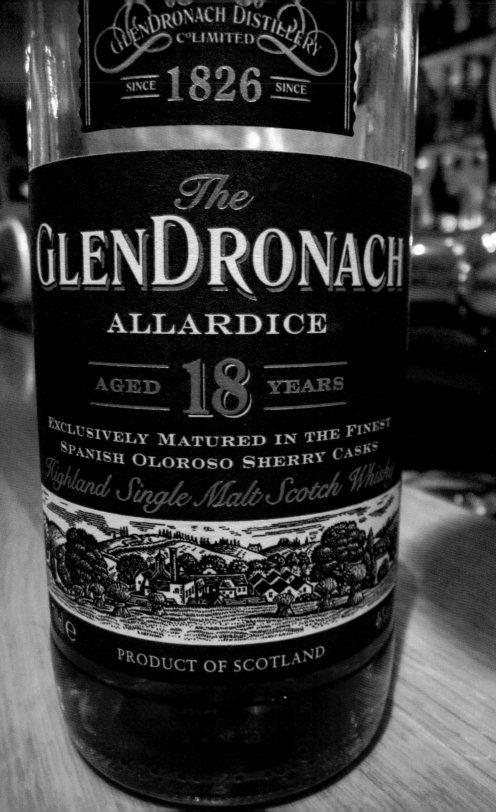

GLENDRONACH ALLARDICE, 18 YEARS OLD (46%)

A COMPOSITE NOSE—slightly exotic fruit, sherry, wine notes, youthful but not harsh spirit, and a mild phenolic peaty aroma. A scent of lilac that develops. Tastes deliciously of apple and orange! Caramel too!

THE PALATE is sweetly fruity and full bodied with an underlying mild phenolic note. Dark chocolate. A rich mellow raisin flavor. The alcohol is prominent without water, and as water is added a milder note of dried fruit emerges: rum and raisin with a slight nutty flavor. There is also a pleasant mild note of cask wine.

THE FINISH is what you would expect of an 18-year-old sherry-aged whisky: a cask-infused, preserve-like sherry flavor, with a delicious phenolic note and well-balanced astringency. A real gem from the chewing gum dispenser in terms of quality for price!

An excellent whisky with both fruit and phenols. Definitely top marks.

STRENGTH ETC. / SCORE: 1 2 3 4 5

NOSE: ....

PALATE: ....

FINISH: ....

GLENFARCLAS 105, 20 YEARS OLD (60%)

THE NOSE HAS SHERRY, candied almonds, and also rather pungent spirit vapors, but the whisky is nonetheless quite mild considering it is 60 percent alcohol. But, of course, luxuriating in a well-chosen oak cask for twenty years can smooth the most stubborn whisky. The original is clearly more volatile and explosive in its nose than this well-rounded chaser. Here there is a slight peat-smoky nuance above a compôte-like fruity note that is compact like Turkish delight. The oak cask note here has a hint of butter.

THE PALATE is brisk and fiery and reveals both the tannin roughness of oak and sherry fruits, with some notes of paper glue. These are not the ordinary sweet sherry notes—breakfast marmalade if you like—but a somewhat more acidic berry-like tone. It has matured in particularly well-chosen casks and the balance is excellent. When I roll it a little on my tongue cayenne pepper also develops and also a note of medium-sweet sherry that has an astringency like chewing grape seeds.

THE FINISH is initially concentrated Speyside. I feel like a smiling Japanese tourist, not the one in the famous story that was locked in overnight at Ardbeg, but one behind the bright red doors on a beautiful night in the Glenfarclas warehouse instead. When I let that thought go, I am surprised by the fact that the aroma softens relatively quickly. In a longer finish it is precisely the taste of the crunchy grape seeds that lingers and a light vanilla-tinged note of fresh juicy raisins.

STRENGTH ETC. / SCORE: 1 2 3 4 5

NOSE: ....

PALATE: ....

FINISH: ....

GLENFARCLAS HERITAGE (40%)

FRUITY and somewhat sharp nose with a slight tone of turpentine and a hint of wet dog. Chihuahua preferably—and it passes quite quickly. Under its initial aromas this relatively young brisk whisky has a faint and promising tone of sherry casks and a slight touch of chewy toffee.

THE PALATE is lively and light with a well-balanced and carboniferous fruity tone with noticeable heat.

THE FINISH initially smacks of young oak and heat. It softens to a rugged yet at the same time mild fruity, sweet and delicious finale, with a hint of licorice. An excellent everyday whisky, and a well-chosen nip to precede a meal. For the cook I mean.

The age of the Heritage is unspecified but probably just a little over school age. Launched in 2011 for the Swedish and French markets only and matured one third in sherry casks and two thirds in bourbon casks. It is recommended as a digestif, but in my opinion the fresh alcohol tone means that it can stimulate the appetite just as much as it can help digest food. As is often the case with Glenfarclas this whisky is also particularly modestly priced.

STRENGTH ETC. / SCORE: 1 2 3 4 5

NOSE: ....

PALATE: ....

FINISH: ....

GLENFARCLAS, 15 YEARS OLD (46%)

A RICH AND BALANCED NOSE with nuances of everything from fruity acidic raisin to sweet grape, a tinge of arrack, and a hint of the sweetness of a coffee chaser. As a base for all of this there is a warm but muffled and slightly woody sugar-sweet cask note.

THE PALATE is sweet malt, fruity with a sherry tone, with increasing fieriness in spite of the constant fruitiness. Very consistent without any outstanding characteristics. Powerfully rich in malt, like a berry fruit compôte with a flavor of sweet roasted malt.

THE FINISH is a direct and fresh sherry flavor—a hint of peat can be detected. Stunning flavor of fresh and aromatic dried fruit with the roughness of tannin and a slowly emerging cask bitterness backed by a cognac-like grapey sweetness even in the finish.

An outstanding 15-year-old. Whisky muscles with a classic character and qualities of a coffee chaser that are as fresh and clear as a wind through an apple orchard in fall. Not to be missed.

STRENGTH ETC. / SCORE: 1 2 3 4 5

NOSE: ....

PALATE: ....

FINISH: ....

GLENFIDDICH, 15 YEARS OLD (40%), FORMERLY "SOLERA RESERVE"

THE NOSE IS FRUITY WITH A SLIGHT WHIFF OF LACTIC ACID. A wonderfully balanced and rich aroma of the sherry's dried fruit, which is present the whole time and is offset by a sweet vanilla scent from the bourbon cask.

THE BODY is thinner than the nose might suggest. A lot of fruitiness and a peppery, malty note.

IN THE EARLY FINISH a slight breath of peat that turns into a long undulation of cask, fruit, and malt which finally slows to a dry and slightly fruity finish that is considerably more austere than the first aroma reveals.

This ambitious Speyside whisky is something of a whisky-maker's test piece. It is aged both in sherry casks made of European oak and in bourbon casks made of American oak, for at least fifteen years. To complete the process 1 or 2 percent of the whisky in the American casks is kept in fresh, uncharred casks of American oak for a period of between a few days and a couple of weeks. This whisky and the sherry-aged whisky are married in the big 3,400-gallon (15 cubic meter) cask, where the blending is allowed to continue for four to six months prior to bottling. The reason for this procedure, and also for the earlier name "Solera Reserve", is that the big cask is always at least half full. That means that what you buy in a bottle always bears traces of both the oldest drops in the cask and the youngest ones that have just been added!

STRENGTH ETC. / SCORE: 1 2 3 4 5

NOSE: ....

PALATE: ....

FINISH: ....

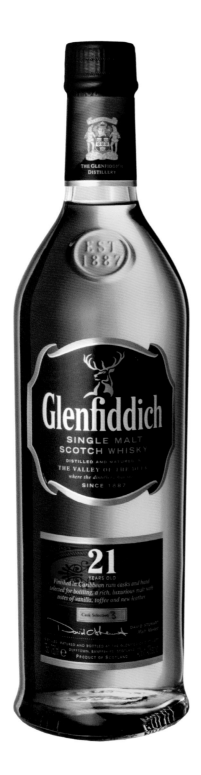

GLENFIDDICH, 21 YEARS OLD (40%), FORMERLY "HAVANA RESERVE"

THE ARRACK TONE IS UNMISTAKABLE, whether you know that it is matured in rum casks or not. A lovely, faint whiff of popcorn is also apparent. The arrack tone together with a spicy tone like allspice, nutmeg, and a little clove produces a very interesting mix, together with the base aroma with its slightly acidic berry-like quality. Like mature blackcurrants marinated in young dark rum.

THE PALATE is fantastically mild and soft. After a short sip the rum notes develop and are then replaced by a consistent malty fruity taste. Somewhere just at the end a hint of peaty smoke comes dancing by and brings with it the finish.

GRADUALLY THE PEAT SMOKE EVAPORATES and a dry moderately long-lasting finish takes over. In the background this has something of both malt and a certain exotic fruitiness. An attractive whisky through and through.

West Indian rum casks from three different countries are used, though it is more than my life is worth to reveal which. I can at least say there is no French rum involved. The maturation in rum casks is a kind of finishing touch of aroma and flavor. The base is sherry and bourbon maturation for at least 21 years followed by storage in rum casks for 3–4 months.

STRENGTH ETC. / SCORE: 1 2 3 4 5

NOSE: ....

PALATE: ....

FINISH: ....

83

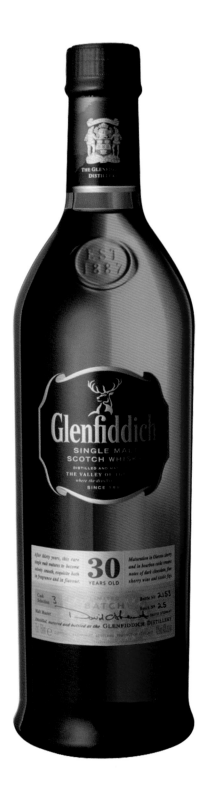

GLENFIDDICH, 30 YEARS OLD (40%)

FIRST A STAB OF SUN-WARMED VARNISH. Then a whirl of acidic fig jam, prunes, and dried dates. Dill, nail polish, and a faint toffee note.

THE PALATE IS BIG, RICH, DIRECT, AND TIGHT LIKE A CLENCHED FIST. A hint of arrack from the maturation but above all a smooth fruitiness in a blend of sweet berry-like and faintly exotic fruits.

THE FINISH begins more fruitily than the younger siblings in the family and becomes increasingly dry. But it still retains a clear fruitiness even quite a while later. Distinguished, balanced, and flavorsome.

Bourbon maturation followed by sherry maturation, but here the portion that is matured in sherry casks at the end is higher than for the 12- and 18-year-olds.

STRENGTH ETC. / SCORE: 1 2 3 4 5

NOSE: ....

PALATE: ....

FINISH: ....

The Spirit Drink
that dare not speak its name

BE INFORMED: this is not Single Malt Scotch Whisky. If for three solitary years we kept it in oak casks in our coastal Highland warehouse it would be, but we simply couldn't wait. This is Glen———gh's New Spirit with all the joy, hope and glamour of life before it, a spirit that is as pure as it is perfect. It is beautiful, it is fine, it is good enough to drink.

50cl Distilled and Bottled by Glenglassaugh Distillery Co. Ltd 50% vol

GLENGLASSAUGH—THE SPIRIT DRINK THAT DARE NOT SPEAK ITS NAME (50%)

THE FIRST IMPRESSION is of citrus and a sweet nose with a tinge of licorice. The combination of aromas and the unmatured alcohol also produces a chili-like sharpness. For a malt distillate straight from the pot it feels unusually light and is almost completely free of oily notes. On the other hand, there is a lightly perfumed freshness and a round sweetness with the accent on the raw barley.

THE PALATE is fiery and sweet. The alcohol makes its presence clearly felt with a burning note that has a lot of fruitiness. There is a hint of pear that gives it the impression of being much more of a German distillate than it actually is. With a little swilling a drier grainy note emerges and a more whisky-like texture.

THE FINISH takes over where the palate ends, even in the character. Soon a note of grain and seed husks also comes through. It is short, dry, and yet balanced in all its simplicity. So, even if this drink does not seem to want to speak its name, it is well worth trying, both in relation to a matured similar one and as an interesting alternative to grappa after dinner!

Launched for the first time in 2009 as an unmatured variant on the traditional fine Glenglassaugh. And the distillery is located in Portsoy, by the way, the little place north of Speyside on the North Sea, where parts of the movie Local Hero *were once shot.*

STRENGTH ETC. / SCORE: 1 2 3 4 5

NOSE: ....

PALATE: ....

FINISH: ....

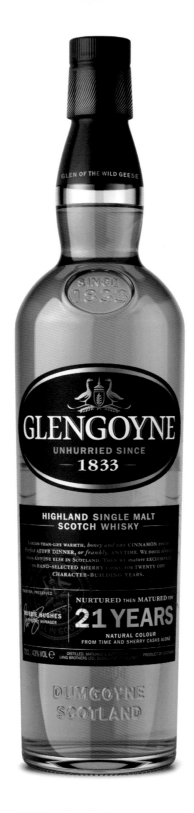

GLENGOYNE, 21 YEARS OLD (43%)

FROM THE VALLEY OF THE GEESE, AS ITS NAME IS SAID TO MEAN IN GAELIC, comes this well-aged, mild, unsmoked whisky. The nose is cask accented and has a sweet note. It smells like the outside of a freshly baked sponge cake with vanilla and a lot of caramel, toffee brittle, and treacle, plus also a little ripe fruit—bananas and melon—and gives the impression of a somewhat higher alcohol content than it actually has.

THE PALATE is richly sweet, but with a clear tautness from the cask. A certain fieriness accelerates but is tempered by the sweetness and is really an asset that ensures that the whole thing does not overflow and become too sweet.

THE FINISH is, like the palate, characterfully sweet with a certain fruiti-ness, and it has a very bread-like vanilla note. A comparison? Well, like a vanilla heart perched on a handful of fruit cocktail, the whole sprinkled with a little crystallized sugar. All told, a chaser with quite a bite yet with all the burnt sweetness, and some of the fruitiness, that a chaser could want.

Now an independent distillery, owned by the independent bottlers Ian MacLeod Distillers. This malt whisky is supposed, at least it was formerly, to have been the main malt in the Famous Grouse. Glengoyne is categorized as a Highland distillery even though it is located so far south that you can reach it in half an hour from Glasgow, so it is well visited by whisky tourists.

STRENGTH ETC. / SCORE: 1 2 3 4 5

NOSE: ....

PALATE: ....

FINISH: ....

89

GLENLIVET NADURRA,
16 YEARS OLD (54.2%)

LYCHEE FRUIT, TUTTI-FRUTTI ICE CREAM, Midori liqueur, melon-flavored sweets, strong vanilla. Creamy—like poking your nose into a pack of vanilla ice cream.

DIRECT COOL VANILLA CREAM in the palate. Somewhat less full bodied than the plump nose suggests. A little added water helps. Vanilla wafer-like flavor with a dryness that is surprisingly strong, yet full and noticeably more astringent and drier without added water.

IN THE FINISH it is soon increasingly vegetable peppery with exotic fruit and vanilla cream elements. Mouth-drying. The finish is medium long and descends toward an unexpected but fresh wood bitterness.

This one can be added to the section on top combinations with coffee. Like Old Pulteney, it is on my top five list of whiskies that masterfully match up to a well-made, full-bodied cappuccino. But do add a little water to Nadurra so that the spirit does not destroy the creamy marriage between the two of them.

This is an unusually good product from an otherwise pretty traditional distillery. Nadurra is Gaelic and is said to mean "natural." This gem is matured only in first-time bourbon oak casks. It is bottled at full strength from the cask without either dilution or cold filtering. More of the same, please!

STRENGTH ETC. / SCORE: 1 2 3 4 5

NOSE: ....

PALATE: ....

FINISH: ....

91

GLENMORANGIE ORIGINAL (40%)

A NOSE OF VANILLA, CITRUS FRUIT, AND ORANGE-FLAVORED CAKE. A little like those childhood wafers filled with vanilla cream. In the background peat and also sweeter fruit, canned peaches, peep through slightly. The nose is dominated by citrus peel, varying from candied peel to a hint of crisply fresh, newly squeezed orange peel.

THE PALATE is at first directly sweet, with balanced maltiness and a freshness that supports the whole. After a little swilling the malt emerges increasingly clearly.

IN THE FINISH THE FRESH FRUITINESS develops into an increasingly dry yet creamy citrus note. The finale is a mild note of butter toffee with a faint malt in the background. A fantastic standard product.

Bourbon cask matured.

STRENGTH ETC. / SCORE: 1 2 3 4 5

NOSE: ....

PALATE: ....

FINISH: ....

GLENMORANGIE, 18 YEARS OLD, "EXTREMELY RARE" (43%)

FLOWERS AND FRUIT: lilac, elderflower, and a couple of tulips in the bower. The fruitiness is sweet and creamy. It resembles butter toffee with a few flaked almonds and a fruit flavor—shall we say strawberry? Many drinks have been described by Carl-Jan as generous, but here the palate would definitely quiver at the delightful invitation that this warm character offers. It smells of—well, I'll be blowed—roses. Rose Turkish delight.

THE PALATE is at first surprisingly smooth and sweet, like a fruity syrup. Soon a little fieriness develops from the spirit and it is also hotted up by the tautness that the casks have imparted during the extra years that this sweetheart has been maturing. Running through the palate the whole time is the solid workmanship with a foundation built on malt and bourbon casks that produces a full, rounded, and slightly bready vanilla sweetness.

THE FINISH is initially bourbon cask and grain. Then a more exotic fruit note also develops that combines well with a flowery rose aroma. When these fleeting scents have evaporated, there remains a warm, slightly rugged taste of sweet fruit. A very inviting scent and an excellent option if you need a coffee stiffener.

The maturation for this whisky is fifteen years in bourbon casks and then a three year finish in sherry casks.

STRENGTH ETC. / SCORE: 1 2 3 4 5

NOSE: ....

PALATE: ....

FINISH: ....

95

GLENMORANGIE

HIGHLAND SINGLE MALT
SCOTCH WHISKY

FINEALTA

PRIVATE EDITION

Finealta (Gaelic for 'elegant') is an exquisite recreation of Glenmorangie as it would have been enjoyed in the early 1900s. Created from an original recipe, Glenmorangie Finealta has distinctive vanilla and citrus notes, and layers of rich fruit flavours from part-maturation in Oloroso sherry casks. Lightly-peated malt adds a surprising hint of subtle smokiness and layers of depth to discover.

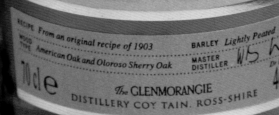

RECIPE From an original recipe of 1903 BARLEY Lightly Peated

WOOD TYPE American Oak and Oloroso Sherry Oak MASTER DISTILLER *W.S.L* Dr Bill Lumsden

70 cl e 46% vol

The GLENMORANGIE
DISTILLERY COY TAIN. ROSS-SHIRE

GLENMORANGIE FINEALTA (46%)

THE NOSE is fruitily perfumed and remarkably composed of prickly sweetness, dried fruit, a little peaty phenols, and even a drop of household glue as well. Dried fruit and vanilla dominate in a vanilla scent that almost reminds you of shortbread.

THE PALATE is at first peppery, especially if at the same time you try one of the others from this family. The pepperiness is matched by a creamy sweetness that has both a malty grain note and a golden edge of phenol the whole time, just like the nose.

THE FINISH begins with phenols that, together with the malty sweetness, are delicious. As they fade a smooth, dry cask note increases and this maintains a malty sweetness that runs through this whisky and soon develops into a longer finish with more of a grain-accented, seed-husk-like character. Unfortunately a one-off, but I hope that demand has ensured that it becomes a permanent fixture. I hope that you and I will find this on the bar shelves for a long while yet.

The Gaelic finealta is said to mean "elegant" in English. According to the maker the formula dates from 1903 and, apart from the slight smoky note, the maturation in oloroso casks clearly contributes to the pleasing fruitiness. Very successful and definitely old and classic, but I wax quite lyrical at the first taste in the mouth—a taste that can only be described as "good whisky" in order not to complicate matters!

STRENGTH ETC. / SCORE: 1 2 3 4 5

NOSE: ....

PALATE: ....

FINISH: ....

GLENMORANGIE SIGNET (46%)

A TOP NOSE THAT, STRANGELY ENOUGH, FIRST MAKES ME THINK OF YOUNG SPIRIT AND WET WOOD. Soon though, a rich note of both oak and burnt sugar emerges, like a gas flame on crème brûlée. Here you find scents of dried fruit, a bourbon-like note of toasted oak, nut brittle, and a hint of dusty maize spirit. Perhaps a scent like canned mandarin segments will come across or otherwise a sweet caramel-like orange scent.

FAINTLY IN THE NOSE AND MORE CLEARLY IN THE PALATE there is also a note of milk chocolate. The character is not at all the bitter, dry, dark chocolate note that is found in older whiskies, contributed by the taste and aroma of oak-cask maturation, but sweet and mild like the milk chocolate you drink. This unusual property comes from the fact that a small percentage of chocolate malt has been stirred into the malt mix, in other words malt that has been roasted harder and acquired the color and taste of chocolate. Apart from this the palate is strongly oak flavored and slightly fruity. It develops into more maltiness with a hint of fresh citrus notes, as in the Glenmorangie Original.

THE FINISH is richly toffee sweet and malty, with the chocolate malt making its presence felt here too. At first it feels like a faint white chocolate flavor. Subsequently it develops into cotton candy, while the malt and a little cask dryness are there in the background. The finish is medium long and like a mix of bourbon and Scotch that gradually rounds off in a drier finale. An unusual whisky with a creative new style that it is well worth spoiling yourself with.

STRENGTH ETC. / SCORE: 1 2 3 4 5

NOSE: ....

PALATE: ....

FINISH: ....

99

HAMMER HEAD

CZECH VINTAGE SINGLE MALT WHIS

THE PRÁDLO DISTILLERY

maturation   100% Czech oak

distillery manager   Václav Šitner

bottled   Prádlo Distillery

malt 100% Czech barley   40.7%

700ml

40.7% vol.

DISTILLED IN
1989

PRODUCT OF
CZECH REPUBLIC

HAMMERHEAD (40.7%)

THIS MUCH TOUTED WHISKY from behind the former Iron Curtain is made in Prádlo, not far from Pilsen. It is a single malt distilled in 1989, the casks were Czech oak, and it lay about twenty years in oblivion in casks before the whisky was bottled a few years ago.

IT SMELLS OF rhubarb and hazelnuts in an aroma that is not as malty and full bodied as a Scotch whisky has accustomed us to expect. There is also a slightly prickly, vanilla sweet note here that is reminiscent of toffee with a touch of honey.

THE PALATE is dry. In spite of the twenty years there is also a fieriness, but there is a good balance with a sweet, candy-like fruitiness. There is ruggedness, but the oak notes are more young and fresh than heavy and astringent.

THE FINISH is toffee-fruity and dry with a perfumed note that develops into licorice root and jelly beans. Not in the least uneven and perhaps a bottle to look out for now as there are rumors that production is to be started up again.

STRENGTH ETC. / SCORE: 1 2 3 4 5

NOSE: ....

PALATE: ....

FINISH: ....

101

HIGHLAND PARK, 12 YEARS OLD (40%)

A HARBOR-ACCENTED NOSE, VERY SLIGHTLY MUSTY. A hint of peat and a little of a freshly ironed shirt. With added water a touch more fruit emerges. What previously tended toward a hint of rubber now becomes a clearer peaty aroma.

THE PALATE is dry and sweet at the same time in a strange way, and is supported by underlying peat smoke. Simple but brilliant.

THE FINISH is very complex, with mild fruit, both fresh and dried. Here too there is an underlying note of peat smoke. This is just how good a 12-year-old whisky can be! Highly recommended.

About 15 percent first-time sherry casks and mainly European oak.

STRENGTH ETC. / SCORE: 1 2 3 4 5

NOSE: ....

PALATE: ....

FINISH: ....

HIGHLAND PARK, 18 YEARS OLD (43%)

RICH FRUITY NOSE, with pear drops, a few dried apricots, and a hint of orange.

THE PALATE HAS AN UNOBTRUSIVE AND WELL-BALANCED SWEET-NESS with a continuing fruity note, and also a bready dryness that gradually releases the peat flavor.

THE PEATY NOTE CONTINUES ON IN THE FINISH, which has light, fruity, almost perfumed, flowery elements that meander on toward peat and casks. Complex and unusually varied in its combination of character traits. A whisky to spoil yourself with, or otherwise a whisky to use to introduce someone to the world of malt whisky—with a great chance of success.

Forty-five percent blended from first-time casks.

STRENGTH ETC. / SCORE: 1 2 3 4 5

NOSE: ....

PALATE: ....

FINISH: ....

HIGHLAND PARK, 25 YEARS OLD, NOT COLD FILTERED (48.1%)

THE NOSE IS HEAVY AND SWEETLY FLOWERY—nectar and honey. With added water it tends to the sweet and fruity side, with elements of lychee and dessert fruit sweetness.

THE PALATE is drier and tauter than expected and balances nicely between fruit, sweetness, and a slightly dill-accented cask character.

THE PEATY FLAVOR IS ALMOST NON-EXISTENT IN THE FINISH, when at first a whiff of smoked herring emerges and then the peat is there as a backdrop, in a long, caramel sweet and slightly fruity but long and tasty finish. Brilliant!

Fifty percent first-time sherry cask.

STRENGTH ETC. / SCORE: 1 2 3 4 5

NOSE: ....

PALATE: ....

FINISH: ....

HIGHLAND PARK, 40 YEARS OLD, NOT COLD FILTERED (48.3%)

WET WOOD, A HAIRSBREADTH FROM BEING OVERMATURED and tired in the woody notes, yet still on the right side, with its remaining strength saving the whole. There is a cognac-like fruitiness in the nose. With a drop of water or two the troubling note of wet wood recedes and the fruit comes to the fore.

IN THE PALATE THERE IS A SOLID FRUITY SWEETNESS that encloses a note of peat. It is more evident here than is the case with the ten-year younger bottling. This whisky is so velvety smooth that it would undoubtedly not need a velour bag with tassels on to sell it even in Kuala Lumpur. Sweet fruit and manifest peat in a very attractive blend.

A FINISH that almost sticks to the tongue in its richness. At bottom peat and on top of that sweet dried fruit that accompanies freshly picked green apples, a hint of burnt vanilla waffles, and then more peat that toward the end fades into a rugged cask-accented but slightly fruity sweet yearning. An obvious candidate amongst the 101 you must drink. And why should such a whisky really need a brand ambassador?

The slightly clearer peaty note in this whisky, in the editions from the beginning of the twenty-first century, is explained by the fact that up to the end of the 1970s the kilning took place entirely in the distillery and that the malt at that time was also somewhat more peat smoked than it was subsequently. Today Highland Park themselves only malt about 20–25 percent of the malt that is used and the rest is bought in.

STRENGTH ETC. / SCORE: 1 2 3 4 5

NOSE: ....

PALATE: ....

FINISH: ....

109

JAMESON SELECT RESERVE / BLACK BARREL
(40%)

THE NOSE is very soft and it gives a feeling of cosy warmth with a sweetness and toffee-like fullness but without any significant vanilla note. There are elements of creamy chocolate truffles laced with whisky chaser, and the note of blackcurrant that is often found in Irish whisky is more integrated into the sweetness here and is inclined to remind you of concentrated raw blackcurrant juice.

THE PALATE initially has a milk-like note and develops into a slightly fiery but yet again malty sweet taste. The typical Irish bourbon cask character with a hint of blackcurrant is there in the background, but well wrapped up in a solid but soft toffee note that envelops the whole thing in a very inviting way.

THE FINISH is at first somewhat spicy and toffee-like and develops into a creamier finale where an initial momentary peak of slightly sharper toffee sauce turns into a slightly berry-like and buttery experience with a final burst of grain. Very much multifaceted and well coordinated.

This whiskey has various names depending on which market you are in, hence the twofold title. This is a blend of pot still whiskey and corn whisky that has been matured in well-chosen bourbon and oloroso sherry casks.

STRENGTH ETC. / SCORE: 1 2 3 4 5

NOSE: ....

PALATE: ....

FINISH: ....

111

JACK DANIEL'S OLD NO. 7 (40%)

THE NOSE is a mixture of dry burnt oak notes with a touch of minerals. There are also sweet and strong fruity aromas, like preserved apricots with desiccated coconut and vanilla ice cream. Somewhere in the transition from crunchy dry oak and fruit there is also a strand of candy-accented maple syrup together with a drop of household glue.

THE PALATE is initially very briefly dry and woody, but it quickly fills out with a burnt fruity sweetness. The oak flavor and a rounded taste of burnt sugar balance well and there is a glimpse of the maize, more like a faint note of popcorn.

THE FINISH takes a step of sweetness before it drops first to a popped maize taste, and that then develops into an increasingly rugged downhill slope of oak with a few wisps of cotton candy and a little seed husk toward the end.

It is difficult to call one of the world's most widely sold spirits underestimated but J.D. deserves a better reputation amongst the many people who turn up their noses at this rock'n'roll whiskey. For me it is the obvious choice for the swing seat in the heat of high summer, with a couple of ice cubes. It tastes just as good at room temperature, perhaps somewhat unexpectedly, with a crispy crème brûlee!

STRENGTH ETC. / SCORE: 1 2 3 4 5

NOSE: ....

PALATE: ....

FINISH: ....

JEFFERSON'S

KENTUCKY STRAIGHT
BOURBON WHISKY
VERY SMALL BATCH

41.2 ALC. VOL.　　　700ML

JEFFERSON'S KENTUCKY STRAIGHT BOURBON (41.2%)

NAIL POLISH, minerals and oak, lychees, and the juice of cherries and raspberries. A fairly light body, but with some significant traits, a witty type, smart and surprising like Sammy Davis Junior on stage.

THE PALATE is at first slightly peppery and fiery, and develops in a mixture of fruity maize notes and apple soda with elements of both raisin and dark berry-fruits. Both elegant and fruity and welcoming in a berry-like way.

THE FINISH is first toffee and oak and topped by a creamy mouth-feel before ebbing away in drier, even slightly salty notes of grain, with a hint of lightly toasted popcorn. A whiskey well worth buying, a discreet and charming gentleman, where the much talked about bourbon bottling from Colorado is the little imp to romp with on the swing seat.

By the way, note that the full name is Jefferson's Kentucky Straight Bourbon Whisky Very Small Batch—the longest in the book and neatly packed with a picture of Mr. Thomas himself printed on the back of the bottle, to be admired by those of us who look deeply into it.

STRENGTH ETC. / SCORE: 1 2 3 4 5

NOSE: ....

PALATE: ....

FINISH: ....

115

JOHNNIE WALKER BLACK LABEL (40%)

THE NOSE has a sharp fiery introduction, but for a blended whisky it is still soft. There is spiciness with notes of aniseed and peppery nuances, freshly mown grass, and a slight toffee aroma.

THE PALATE is almost creamily smooth to begin with. As if on a bridge of malty sweetness it then develops toward a more astringent grain note with warming pepperiness, sweet fruit, and butter toffee. Saltiness and a faint smokiness are there in the background, from the malt types that contribute these character traits.

THE FINISH is medium long but has an attractive dryness that balances well with light fruity sweetness that also has a hint of arrack. The whole ends with a slightly bitter and sugar-sweet finale that perhaps reflects what it says on the label: "color adjusted with caramel."

This whisky is a very good standard whisky for the price. It is also a safe bet to give away—good enough to be drunk by a whisky lover but also good enough to pass on to anyone who has not yet learnt to like it …!

STRENGTH ETC. / SCORE: 1 2 3 4 5

NOSE: ....

PALATE: ....

FINISH: ....

KAVALAN SINGLE MALT WHISKY (40%)

THE NOSE is compact but mild. A balanced, burnt sugar note dominates; it smells like well-made, caramelized hard toffee that has been cooked for a long time, with undertones of both cream toffee and coconut. I also sense a hint of lychee, and there is a whiff of marzipan with a mango jam filling. The aroma has a feather-light nuance of smoke and saltiness, something that reminds me of the colors of the sea and emerald green. Exciting, intricate, and not too old.

THE PALATE is very smooth and discreet as it emerges. It is almost bordering on watery, but nonetheless it has sherry aromas that wrestle with a slight but robust hint of butter toffee. The butter toffee wins. The fieriness increases somewhat and is filled out with a balanced, mature oak note, and a soft, nutty chocolate toffee flavor.

THE FINISH has a direct sherry topping that passes. Faint grain fights with slightly warming notes and raisins, with a pinch of licorice, in a medium-long finale. Like many before me, I can tell that the Kavalan whisky has put Taiwan on the whisky map, and decisively so. This one is good.

This is a standard malt from King Car I-Lan Distillery who make Kavalan. Other versions are various wine maturations, amongst others fino sherry and bourbon-matured variants such as single cask in full-cask strength, in the Kavalan Solist series.

STRENGTH ETC. / SCORE: 1 2 3 4 5

NOSE: ....

PALATE: ....

FINISH: ....

KILBEGGAN, 18 YEARS OLD (40%)

THE NOSE is quite clearly a substantial ladle full of bourbon. There can be no doubt as to how this top Irish whiskey is matured. However there is an oily note in the aroma that provides a slightly more muted impression and that rounds down the sometimes rather sharp oak note that you find in an authentic bourbon. For an 18-year-old whiskey it has a clear alcohol note but not to a disturbing degree. The aroma is creamier and has a touch of alcohol, something reminiscent of the aromatic impression of a certain cream liqueur. There is also a certain mature fruitiness, a bit like that of a really ripe netted melon, sweet and dripping with fruitiness.

THE FIRST THING THAT STRIKES ME IN THE PALATE IS HOW TREMENDOUSLY SMOOTH IT IS. Extremely creamy and with a growing malty sweetness. The bourbon note is milder and the balance between malt and cask is superb.

IN THE FINISH ITS ORIGINS MAKE THEMSELVES FELT just briefly. A wave of blackcurrant leaves washes over the tongue and a slightly oily note of malt with a certain appetizing fieriness remains. About half a minute later there is just a slightly vanilla-accented toffee aroma with clear traits of semi-dry maltiness. Without doubt a future favorite coffee chaser that calls out for a mild robusto cigar and a white chocolate truffle with a pear filling!

STRENGTH ETC. / SCORE: 1 2 3 4 5

NOSE: ....

PALATE: ....

FINISH: ....

121

KILCHOMAN WINTER 2010 RELEASE VERSUS MACHIR BAY

Two from the westernmost Scottish distillery —one of the youngest. The Kilchoman farm distillery on the west coast of Islay makes 26,000 gallons (100,000 liters) of whisky a year. It is a gem that is developing nicely. Here is a mini sampling suited to the armchair in front of the TV.

WINTER 2010 RELEASE (46%)

THE NOSE IS SWEETLY SMOKY and reminds me of licorice root and a fruity barbecue glaze. It is reminiscent of burnt reeds and very faintly of plastic. With added water it is softer, smoother, and has greater sweetness. Quite a simple taste with direct smokiness, a sweet but young spirit with a touch of cask ruggedness but more fieriness. Filled with vegetable bitterness and also a hint of marzipan. The finish is grassy and astringent and has a sweet nutty, almond note that develops into more of a grain flavor. Young, astringent, and sweetly smoky.

Blended from whiskies matured in refill and new bourbon casks.

MACHIR BAY 2012 (46%)

A FLOWERY BERRY-LIKE NOSE—rose and geranium, and sweet licorice, modeling clay, and boiled vegetables. Milder and rounder than the winter release. The nose becomes milder and creamier with added water, and is reminiscent of lemon curd—and a hint of modeling clay! The palate is peppery and fruity, at first more like green apples. This develops into a faint raisin note wrapped in a fiery and medium-bodied sweetness with a little modeling clay in the taste. Toward the end more strawberry-jam-like sherry cask notes. The finish is faintly sherry tinged with astringency tending toward chocolate. Shortly after there is a strong licorice taste—big, dark brown pieces. This gives way to a new guise, as it gradually fades away into a sunset of licorice-spiced grain.

Made from a mixture of whisky matured for three, four, and five years. The 4-year-old is finally matured for eight weeks in sherry butts.

KNOB CREEK, 9 YEARS OLD (50%)

A STRONG NOSE COMPRISING FRUIT COMPÔTE WITH DILL VAPORS, in which the high alcohol content contributes to a chemical note as if of nail varnish. However this fades away after a brief moment. At bottom there is a scent reminiscent of limestone wet with rain that is drying in the sun. There is a scent of really sweet butter toffee, toffee that has got stuck to the roof of the mouth, together with a burnt-oak scent. An aromatic experience rich in contrasts, between coarsely hewn cask wood and a ladylike perfumed note. The strength means that this bourbon allows both a dash of water and, if the weather so requires, a scoop of crushed ice too.

A FULL-BODIED PALATE in which the fruit mixture spreads through the mouth and a toffee-sauce-like note is held in check by the oak character. There is an attack of rye-like ruggedness and the whiskey also gets some backbone from the alcohol itself.

THE FINISH begins with a syrupy note. It soon develops into a somewhat perfumed medium-long palate that is filled with sweetness. Lightly burnt maize develops into a popcorn note. This produces a sweetness on the tongue and a lip-smacking moreish feeling inside the cheeks.

It can be good to drink on the sofa while watching a movie, with popcorn and a toffee and caramel gateau, or a bite of coconut chocolate!

One of the Jim Beam Group's premium products, with a touch more maize and an even fruitier and more rounded base that combines with a stronger cask character than its siblings Basil Hayden, Booker's et al.

STRENGTH ETC. / SCORE: 1 2 3 4 5

NOSE: ....

PALATE: ....

FINISH: ....

125

LABEL 5 (40%)

THE NOSE is so creamy that it feels almost as if someone has wafted a Baileys in front of your nostrils. However the nose is somewhat sharper—more like a Baileys spiked with toffee-like buttery blended whisky?

THE PALATE is slightly prickly but smoothly vanilla flavored like butter ball candies and creamy like the center of a chocolate with a toffee filling. Unique and, in spite of the endearing buttery patisserie note, there is a big enough pinch of a spirituous sting to hold the structure together so that it does not collapse into a nauseating morass of sloppy sweetness. After you have swilled it for a moment, the extremes of this character are reinforced as a malty, slightly smoky, toffee sweetness takes its place in one corner of the ring while an invigorating fiery spirit note dances impatiently in the other.

THE FINISH is first a topping of malty sensations that slowly and with dignity flatten out into increasingly dry grain nuances with no sweetness. A whiff of vanilla is left in the medium-long finish but held in check by a dry and slightly astringent note from the fine spirit in this extremely smooth yet balanced blend. Long afterward there is also a brisk taste of licorice root that pops out and says "Hi!" Delicious.

STRENGTH ETC. / SCORE: 1 2 3 4 5

NOSE: ....

PALATE: ....

FINISH: ....

LAGAVULIN, 16 YEARS OLD (43%)

A SCENT OF OILSKINS FULL OF FABRIC PLASTERS and with that a consistent, sweetly wet, and tarred bit of hemp rope. Balanced, not at all as flowery as, for instance, Bowmore—even though there is a tinge of slightly more perfumed peat smoke in the midst of the heavy and rather muted tarriness.

THE PALATE is cool and flatteringly spirituous for its age. The smokiness that is well preserved despite sixteen years in the cask quickly increases. A little of burnt popcorn may reveal that bourbon casks are involved. The fullness of the mouth-feel gradually increases.

DIRECTLY IN THE FINISH THERE IS A WOODY, PEPPER-HOT, SMOKY NOTE too, like chili combined with a taste of ham smoked over alder shavings. A dryness emerges and remains. On top of that there is a creamy smooth smokiness that lingers on a long time and develops into an increasingly sweet smokiness. An extremely good, big seller. Strangely enough not something that can be called middle of the road, not even after more than twenty years since it landed in the Six Classic Malts series.

STRENGTH ETC. / SCORE: 1 2 3 4 5

NOSE: ....

PALATE: ....

FINISH: ....

LAPHROAIG QUARTER CASK (48%)

THE LOVELY, SWEET TARRY NOSE that once again reminds you of the sweetness of tarred hemp rope comes through immediately and it combines with a sharper chemical scent, like a few drops of chemically pure gasoline. There is a hint of play-dough clay in the nose, in culinary terms also mixed with marzipan. The whole wafts away at first in a scent of dressings and iodine-treated fabric plasters and then it lands in the scent of marzipan gateau thrown into a rowing boat filled with rope.

THE PALATE IS RICH AND OILY, SWEET, AND PEATY—a buttery peatiness and also bread—like a slice of French bread and a bit of peat in the toaster.

THE FINISH is round and peppery with a certain creaminess, without being at all sickly. It rolls like the waves on the sea in breaker after breaker with salt-soaked sweet peaty smoke and coal-tar pastilles, and subsides gradually into a cask-accented, dry, and still very mild yet sweet, perfumed smokiness. Young, characterful, and balanced, even if the sound volume is turned up quite high in this smoky melody.

This whisky is matured for a number of years in standard casks and then trans-ferred to quarter casks. Hence the name, and note that these are 132-gallon (500-liter) quarter casks. This means that in spite of an unspecified age of something less than ten years it has a very rich character.

STRENGTH ETC. / SCORE: 1 2 3 4 5

NOSE: ....

PALATE: ....

FINISH: ....

LAPHROAIG, 10 YEARS OLD, CASK STRENGTH (55.3%)

THE NOSE is sweet and creamily smoky, with a complex smokiness that reminds you most of food—glazed, smoked duck, or something like that—together with a solid, creamy, yet light spiciness. With added water the nose tends more toward a sweet Cuprinol note that does not retain the food nuance but acquires more of a gunpowder or coal-like smokiness that I find very attractive.

THE PALATE is initially a fiery attack of sweet smokiness. With added water the palate is ruggedly spicy with noticeably less smokiness, even though the oak has left a lot of ruggedness in this whisky, which is only ten years old. The mouth-feel is medium bodied and has a slight note of perfume, almost tending toward lavender.

THE FINISH without added water is tasty like the palate but quite sharp. The character is gasoline-like and sweetly smoky. With added water the finish is like 99 percent chocolate, licorice, and especially a small piece of salt-coated sweet licorice found in the pocket of an oilskin that has been hanging in the wardrobe with a lavender bag. The end of this long chipotle-like finish is tinged with a faint cask bitterness and is pleasantly smoky with a note of licorice. An excellent 10-year-old that can be blended—by you—to a pleasant strength and taste.

STRENGTH ETC. / SCORE: 1 2 3 4 5

NOSE: ....

PALATE: ....

FINISH: ....

LAPHROAIG®

ISLAY SINGLE MALT
SCOTCH WHISKY

AGED **18** YEARS

THIS EXPRESSION OF OUR FAMOUS WHISKY IS MADE IN LIMITED
QUANTITIES EACH YEAR, ONLY TO BE SAVOURED BY A FORTUNATE FEW.
A SOFT AND SPICY ISLAY PEAT SMOKE GREETS YOU WHEN YOU
FIRST OPEN THE BOTTLE, FOLLOWED BY A TASTE OF OAK SWEETNESS
GAINED FROM 18 YEARS MATURING IN AN EX-BOURBON BARREL.

The most richly flavoured of all
Scotch whiskies

ESTᴰ **1815** ESTᴰ

...LED AND BOTTLED IN SCOTLAND
...TON & CO., LAPHROAIG DISTILLERY,
ISLE OF ISLAY

48% vol.

On bottle label:

LAPHROAIG®

ISLAY SINGLE MALT
SCOTCH WHISKY

AGED **18** YEARS

THIS EXPRESSION OF OUR FAMOUS WHISKY IS MATURED
FOR 18 YEARS FOR GREATER DEPTH, TASTE AND TEXTURE

The most richly flavoured of all Scotch whiskies

ESTᴰ 1815 ESTᴰ

DISTILLED AND BOTTLED IN SCOTLAND BY
D. JOHNSTON & CO., LAPHROAIG DISTILLERY, ISLE OF ISLAY

70cl ℮   48% vol.

LAPHROAIG, 18 YEARS OLD (48%)

THE NOSE is very rounded, rich, and full bodied, and of course there is a phenolic peaty note. It also has both a couple of scoops of vanilla and a pinch of manure. There is a meaty saltiness, like smelling pata negra or parma ham, and with it a scent of black olives. What a great whisky for tapas!

THE PALATE is fiery and sweet with a hint of arrack.

THE FINISH has a sugary sweetness and a tarry sweet smokiness. The balance between them is good and as time passes they both persist—what increases is mainly a certain licorice-flavored saltiness. The length of the finish means that I enjoy savoring it a bit longer and hesitate to take the next sip as the goodness really lasts a long time. Sweet, now slightly cask-flavored, and faintly peppery, peat smoke …

—But what in the heck! Cheers again.

STRENGTH ETC. / SCORE: 1 2 3 4 5

NOSE: ....

PALATE: ....

FINISH: ....

LAPHROAIG, 25 YEARS OLD (45.1%)

THE TOP NOSE is slightly musty, but soon a very full and balanced nose that does hold the expected smoke aromas but gives off sweetness, arrack, and slightly meatier scents come through. There is no suggestion of spirit in spite of the high alcohol content.

THE PALATE is at first salty but quickly brings in an arrack-accented sweetness that has a certain fieriness. This is filled out and becomes a touch smoother although it is still sharp.

THE FINISH is, like the nose, a fantastic mixture of fruity sweetness and salt-soaked smokiness, with a note of peat and licorice toffee. In terms of time it will probably last until the next day's breakfast and what is great is that what increases toward the end is more the vanilla and butteriness than the smoke. But, believe me, the smoke is there.

It has been matured in a mixture of American bourbon casks and Spanish oloroso sherry casks.

STRENGTH ETC. / SCORE: 1 2 3 4 5

NOSE: ....

PALATE: ....

FINISH: ....

EST
1798

LEDAIG

AGED 10 YEARS
SINGLE MALT SCOTCH WHISKY
WONDERFULLY PEATED

THE ISLE OF MULL

Distilled and Bottled by Tobermory Distillers Limited

ISLE OF MULL

46.3%Vol. 70cl e

LEDAIG, 10 YEARS OLD (46.3%)

THE NOSE has a familiar, slightly musty note, a little reminiscent of the younger Isle of Jura. The difference compared with many lesser bottlings of Ledaig however is that this one has balance. The mustiness also has a faint burnt note with a tinge of smoked cheese. I can feel both a hint of peat and something slightly similar to the sweet burnt note in grilled bell peppers. The balance comes from the fact that there is an ethereal aroma here that freshens up the mustiness of the peat and that seems to provide rather a scent of rose geranium or pelargonium, yet also has a very attractive sea-like coolness. As I breathe out is there also a strange, very faint note reminiscent of the swimming baths?!

THE PALATE is at first sweetly rounded malt with a slightly cheese-like undertone. It develops into less fullness but has a good balance of sweetness and alcohol, and these are reinforced with a firm young note of smoke.

THE FINISH is elegantly peaty; it has an almost electric vigor that with sweet malt, saltiness, and alcohol in equal parts produces a very pleasant and softly fading finish with a final murmur of some toffee and mineral water. Delicate.

STRENGTH ETC. / SCORE: 1 2 3 4 5

NOSE: ....

PALATE: ....

FINISH: ....

139

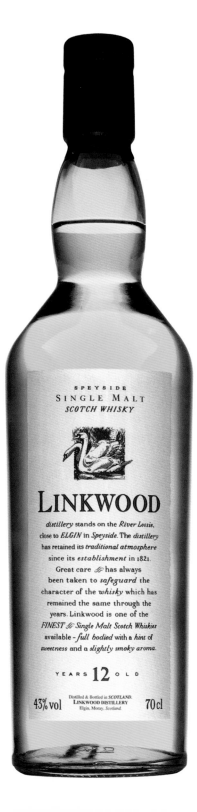

SPEYSIDE
SINGLE MALT
SCOTCH WHISKY

LINKWOOD

distillery stands on the *River Lossie*,
close to *ELGIN* in *Speyside*. The *distillery*
has retained its *traditional atmosphere*
since its *establishment* in 1821.
Great care *&* has always
been taken to *safeguard* the
character of the *whisky* which has
remained the same through the
years. Linkwood is one of the
FINEST *&* *Single Malt Scotch Whiskies*
available - *full bodied* with a hint of
sweetness and a *slightly smoky aroma.*

YEARS **12** OLD

43% vol

Distilled & Bottled in *SCOTLAND*.
LINKWOOD DISTILLERY
Elgin, Moray, *Scotland*.

70 cl

LINKWOOD, 12 YEARS OLD (43%)

A PEPPERY AND ETHER-LIKE spirituous nose that is filled out with the scent of Turkish delight with a rose flavor and a lot of confectioner's sugar. Wood and a few plasticky rubber notes. Sweet with a scent of buttered pancake with vanilla sugar on.

THE PALATE is fiery, peppery, and beneath that has an almost cognac-like fruitiness and a balanced sweetness. It develops into a more full-bodied, smoother character and the whole time it has a base in a mild oak cask note.

THE FINISH is medium dry and with an equally smooth fruity and grape-like note. Toward the end a malty cask-accented rugged taste increases, with a hint of vanilla cream. This is not a wolf in sheep's clothing but it is a whisky in cognac clothing.

STRENGTH ETC. / SCORE: 1 2 3 4 5

NOSE: ....

PALATE: ....

FINISH: ....

141

LONGMORN, 16 YEARS OLD (48%)

A LONG UNDERRATED WHISKY that, with its simple packaging and reasonable price, occasionally crept into the cart when walking round the liquor store. Now it has been relaunched in a much more trendy outfit that looks as though the marketing department was given free rein on a Friday afternoon. A metal collar on the neck and a finely stitched leather-trimmed base. Attractive, but what about the content? Well, yes, to my mind the nose is more strongly fruity than before. The typical apple note is there but more in the style of an apple soda now, with more dried fruit, a little dark marmalade, and yet with a very fine balance between oak cask and a buttery note that softens it.

THE PALATE is very full and soft. The alcohol sets in and also the oak cask note tightens before it subsides again and my thoughts of apple soda are back again in the palate as well. A bitter tannin note comes through toward the end.

THE FINISH is first dry grain notes and veers into the sugar avenue before it turns again into a side street with a faintly vanilla-accented cask character and a residual whiff of pears. Good whisky from the heart of Speyside, but I can't help thinking a little of mixers too. Wouldn't it be nice with apple soda, a slice of apple, and a few ice cubes?

STRENGTH ETC. / SCORE: 1 2 3 4 5

NOSE: ....

PALATE: ....

FINISH: ....

THE MACALLAN FINE OAK, 10 YEARS OLD (40%)

A "SWEET AND SOUR" MALTY NOSE WITH A FAINT VANILLA NOTE.
A whiff of lingonberry jam? Something of warm wood, reminiscent of the
first impression of the smell when you step into your old sun-warmed
weekend cottage and warm hardboard is what greets you.

THE PALATE is a smiling, rounded, sweet note, stylishly balanced with a
faint sourness that develops into a toffee note that is dry but pleasant, and
in its turn is offset well by the malt.

THE FINISH has a light burnt note from the roasting of the American
casks. The taste is long and characterful with a balance between malty
sweetness and cask ruggedness, with a very mild background note of
fruitiness. An unsmoked 10-year-old malt whisky can hardly be better.

STRENGTH ETC. / SCORE: 1 2 3 4 5

NOSE: ....

PALATE: ....

FINISH: ....

THE MACALLAN FINE OAK, 18 YEARS OLD (43%)

TOAST AND MARMALADE—the Scottish way, with lots of orange peel. A buttery aroma. With added water the fruitiness increases and in the background there is a flowery scent, edged with the burnt note.

THE PALATE is extremely well balanced between malty sweetness, ruggedness from the cask, and fruit.

IN THE FINISH a burnt note surprises you here too and the greater age tautens the long finish more than in the younger siblings. An excellent chaser for anyone who thinks that cognac goes off the rails in an all-too-sweet direction.

Roughly speaking the 18-year-old contains half American oak, of which 35 percent is American bourbon casks. There is a major element of European oak from the maturation of this whisky, which is why the color is so strong. It is worth mentioning that about one third is from American casks that have been treated with bourbon and/or sherry. The rest are European sherry casks.

STRENGTH ETC. / SCORE: 1 2 3 4 5

NOSE: ....

PALATE: ....

FINISH: ....

THE MACALLAN FINE OAK, 30 YEARS OLD (43%)

THE IMMEDIATE NOSE here is somewhat more muted than in the younger siblings and that is as befits the age. Like an older cognac it has a fruity nose that is dominated by a heavy sweetness. A drop or two of water causes more fruit and also noticeable vanilla to emerge. There is a certain element of acidity here too, something approaching the sourness in a well-made toffee sauce.

THE PALATE is very mild and smooth, with a cask-matured ruggedness that instantly papers the mouth as the whisky enters it. The palate is compact, very coherent, and in addition to the obvious aspects such as full-bodied malt and burnt sugar notes there is a flowery hint of burnt spiciness that is reminiscent of bourbon casks, sherry, and something that hovers between a pinch of nutmeg and allspice. Gratifyingly there is a spirituous note that adds vigor to this gem.

THE FINISH is strikingly mild, yet rich. Here is the cask ruggedness too, but more reticent than expected in such an old whisky. A note of fruity sweetness balances the ruggedness of the burnt sugar and cask character. A particularly meditative, and indeed actually navel-gazing whisky experience. Drink it on your own. Otherwise your friends might have a go at you …

STRENGTH ETC. / SCORE: 1 2 3 4 5

NOSE: ....

PALATE: ....

FINISH: ....

THE MACALLAN, 12 YEARS OLD (43%)

MILDLY ACIDIC AND CLEARLY FRUITY VANILLA. Well-integrated apple and sweetness.

THE PALATE is round, rich, and fruity with a slowly increasing ruggedness.

THE FINISH is astringently vegetable but borne up on the sweetness of sherry. Vanilla toffee comes through toward the end, not in an ingratiating way but in an overall pleasant finish that lasts a very long time and in the end flutters away toward fruity sweetness and a whiff of a newly ironed cotton shirt. To give a commendatory parallel to the final comment on the 10-year-old Fine Oak—a sherry-matured 12-year-old whisky doesn't come much better than this!

STRENGTH ETC. / SCORE: 1 2 3 4 5

NOSE: ....

PALATE: ....

FINISH: ....

151

THE MACALLAN, 18 YEARS OLD (43%)

TAKE DRIED FRUIT: a few apricots, a couple of plums, a handful of raisins, and a sliver of bitter orange peel for a muted citrus aroma—all waft faintly with allspice and stirred together with golden syrup and molasses. That would produce something approaching the nose of this malt whisky classic. Add to this also a light burnt note tending toward phenol-scented peat smoke.

THE PALATE IS A KNOCK-OUT with a compact character. Balanced sweetness and fruit that is noticeably less cask astringent than its age might lead you to believe. The clear but not excessive, rich, creamy fruit sweetness is what dominates.

THE FINISH is spicily fruity like an oriental fruit salad with mango, lychees, a little pineapple, and a few bits of orange and grape, sprinkled with a little nutmeg and a tiny hint of pepper. On top perhaps a crushed Italian amaretto biscuit to provide a little vanilla-tinged nuttiness. As you can tell, a whisky with a lot of power of association. Forget the cognac. Take this instead.

STRENGTH ETC. / SCORE: 1 2 3 4 5

NOSE: ....

PALATE: ....

FINISH: ....

THE MACALLAN,
WHISKY MAKER'S EDITION (42.8%)

THE NOSE IS CHEEKILY SPIRITUOUS, but with an underlying fresh, rich, and typically malt whisky character. Unusually strong notion of a moped-riding teenager considering the otherwise maturely dominant Macallan character. Geranium. Walnut. Oak. Peppermint toffee.

THE PALATE is very fresh and young without being blatantly immature. Absolutely to my taste as an eternal romantic where spirits are concerned. Gradually a blue-black berry fruitiness emerges, accompanied by a mild, sweet maltiness. The whole thing is reinforced by a very light, well-balanced fieriness, and a youthful charm that slowly fades as the malt takes over and the whole finishes with a creamy blackcurrant flavor.

THE FINISH is a continuation, in a milder variant, of the finale of the palate—creamy like a mousse made of blackcurrants and perhaps a semi-ripe turpentine-imbued mango. The mouth-feel is exceptionally smooth and warm like a cuddly lie-in on a Sunday morning. As a great fan of phenol, I did not think I could fall so much in love with a Speyside whisky, but this is one of the better ones I have tasted. Young, balanced, rich, and unbelievably charming in an exciting variety of endearing and astringent character traits.

This whisky was launched as a tax-free product in 2009. It was one of a series of four bottlings on the theme of 1824, the year when the distillery was founded. The dearest of the four was therefore released in an edition of 1824 bottles, in an expensive crystal carafe.

STRENGTH ETC. / SCORE: 1 2 3 4 5

NOSE: ....

PALATE: ....

FINISH: ....

MACKMYRA FIRST EDITION (46.1%)

THE NOSE is fresh and sweet, almost like a cask-strength Speyside whisky, but with a lower alcohol content. Vanilla wafers, lingonberries and dried apricots, and a touch of fresh woody notes. Together they make up an attractive aroma that has subtle hints of gasoline—as when someone in an oilskin jacket is sitting on a chair opposite. The fruit and the element of vanilla from the wood make me think of raspberry bushes. Not Peat Monster, but definitely cake monster …

THE PALATE is malty, quite austere, and it too is fresh, in spite of its palpable sweetness and full-bodied mouth-feel. Both a peppery and a fiery note gradually emerge. Cask wood and malt balance well, thanks to the fact that both are fairly loud. The—to my mind—typical intense oak note and light ester-like fruits are both present.

THE FINISH is intensely sweet with a rising note of both seed husks and fresh wood that gradually develops more dominance from the woody note and also tastes a little of well-chewed licorice root toward the end. With the growing woody note a very, very mild smoky note also emerges.

STRENGTH ETC. / SCORE: 1 2 3 4 5

NOSE: ....

PALATE: ....

FINISH: ....

-ISLAY-ISLAY- -ISLAY-ISLAY

estab. 1934

MACLEOD'S

ISLAY
SINGLE MALT
SCOTCH WHISKY

PRODUCED AND BOTTLED BY
IAN MACLEOD AND CO LTD. EH52 5BU

Product of Scotland

40%vol. / 70cl.

91245

MACLEOD'S ISLAY (40%)

THIS UNNAMED SINGLE MALT from Islay is better value for money than many other whiskies for winter use. This blinder brings somewhat jaded senses back to life and thaws your fingers after a ski tour in the snow in January. The nose has a young, sharp sweetness with notes of cigarette ash and a hint of egg toddy.

THE PALATE is full and round, and the alcohol is not obvious, even though the character is young and straightforward. A fantastic balance between slightly peppery, fiery alcohol, and malty sweetness, with a clear but rounded smokiness.

THE FINISH has elements of licorice root, with just the balance of alcohol and a slightly caramel-accented round smoky note that has however barely reached adolescence, but in terms of age is more likely working on qualifying for middle school. And it is precisely that that is its asset—this is an incredibly well-picked whisky, albeit anonymous in so far as the maker is unknown. In spite of that it is full of qualities, especially considering the price tag!

STRENGTH ETC. / SCORE: 1 2 3 4 5

NOSE: ....

PALATE: ....

FINISH: ....

MAKER'S MARK (43%)

A HINT OF A HOT SPIRITUOUS NOSE brings out candy aromas like jelly beans and raspberry ribbons. There is a touch of cherry juice and raisins in combination with sweet burnt oak and a little ethyl acetate. The aroma of burnt wood also produces a mineral note like rain-wet stone.

THE PALATE is sharp but full bodied and oaken, and the candy-like note in the nose stays in the background here, behind a solidly full-bodied and balanced burnt note of a little oak and a lot of brittle-toffee-like sweetness. After a moment's swilling the oak note develops and becomes more dominant, and also acquires an element of grain.

THE FINISH is dry and at the same time perfumed and aromatic with a lot of the candy note that was present in the nose. In a long but light finish there is a hint of oak and even more crispy burnt sugar.

This bourbon has the unusual feature that the recipe contains wheat as the third base material, together with maize and barley. Usually rye is used as the third ingredient. Using wheat produces a slightly milder taste. The maturation time of about seven years also produces a good balance between dryness and sweetness in this good-value bourbon that works at least as well in a long drink as neat.

STRENGTH ETC. / SCORE: 1 2 3 4 5

NOSE: ....

PALATE: ....

FINISH: ....

161

MICHTER'S SMALL BATCH AMERICAN WHISKEY (41.7%)

THE NOSE is sweet and candy-like with a note of rye, and also a mixture of jelly beans, fruit pastilles, and oak—mild but aged and wrapped in sweetness. Fascinating nods to oak timber and candy bags, and to powdered marshmallows and vanilla ice cream with strawberry sauce.

THE PALATE IS FIRST WOOD, with a flourish of well-matured Scotch whisky and a topping of burnt popcorn. An aged, dry, oakwood taste is immediate. The dryness persists, even if it is filled out with a sweeter vanilla powdered taste that nicely balances the dryness.

THE FINISH IS SOUR AND SLIGHTLY RUGGEDLY OAKY. The corn taste is there in the background—as after a mouthful of popcorn—and increases steadily, while the sweetness is faint and the aroma of caramel marginal. After a long, dry, and mildly oaky finish a handful of well-warmed buttered popcorn lingers on. The nose in itself gives wings to the mysterious but characterful American made from mixed ingredients.

Founded in 1753 in Schaefferstown, PA, and the USA's oldest distillery when closed in 1978. The whisky sampled is bottled in Bardstown, KY, possibly like some older bottlings from residual stock from the company's liquidation in 1992. In the same distillery A.H. Hirsch whiskey was pot distilled. Michter's was made more traditionally in four-step columns and then a doubler. The base material is 10 percent barley malt and 45 percent each of rye and corn, which does not comply with the over-51 percent corn required for a bourbon—hence the name.

STRENGTH ETC. / SCORE: 1 2 3 4 5

NOSE: ....

PALATE: ....

FINISH: ....

NAKED GROUSE (40%)

PARTICULARLY ATTRACTIVE PACKAGING, with a red grouse embossed on the glass and apart from that no label except round the neck of the bottle. The nose has an evident Scottish stamp, a few toffee notes, and a faint smoke that provides a taut but slightly salty fruitiness, like raisins and salted roasted almonds.

THE PALATE has a note of dried fruit, raisins, and also malt. There is a certain heat that comes from the alcohol, but the slightly salty bread note returns in the palate. One clear trait is also a dry, rugged, oak background tone.

THE FINISH TOO has a high level of ruggedness from the cask maturation, and even though this whisky does not have an age specified, you can feel that it has a clear element of a more oak-accented part in the mix of malts. Naked as it is called, and like a plucked goose somewhat cold, but in its tautness it is a suitable candidate if you want a good Scotch before dinner—especially as nuts, raisins, and pretzels are already there in the nose and the palate!

This blend of malts, like the Famous Grouse, has a significant element of the Glenrothes Speyside whisky and also of the famous Highland Park. Forty percent of the casks are used for the first time, with the bulk of the casks being made of European oak that has held oloroso sherry. The ages of the whiskies it comprises are up to eight years.

STRENGTH ETC. / SCORE: 1 2 3 4 5

NOSE: ....

PALATE: ....

FINISH: ....

NIKKA
COFFEY GRAIN
WHISKY

PRODUCED BY THE NIKKA WHISKY
DISTILLING CO., LTD., JAPAN

カフェグレーン

alc.45%　　ウイスキー　　50〜
NIKKA WHISKY

NIKKA COFFEY GRAIN (45%)

Distilled in column stills and with maize up to 95.4 percent, then matured in American oak casks and composed from different casks with whisky that is not more than twelve years old. That is the background to this very delicate and palatable whisky.

THE NOSE has elements of arrack and soft vanilla and there is also a faintly rose-like floweriness. The slightly chemical note, like a mixture of household glue and a little packing tape, drifts away and does not affect the score.

THE PALATE is at first rounded and very full bodied. A soft feel develops into a more fiery character and what from the beginning was full of arrack develops into an increasingly fruity acquaintance.

TO BEGIN WITH THE FINISH is highly reminiscent of Irish whiskey, with a note of blackcurrant, and this is most probably due to the production process and the base material. In the longer finish a faint note of cream toffee emerges and with that a note of licorice root. The finish is relatively short but makes the point once again that you can put an equals sign between balance and Japanese whisky.

STRENGTH ETC. / SCORE: 1 2 3 4 5

NOSE: ....

PALATE: ....

FINISH: ....

NIKKA ALL MALT (40%)

A FEW BOURBON CASK NOTES, a little sweet exotic fruit, and a dash of lychee juice. There is also an aroma that is reminiscent of fresh cream. And then a mineral-accented, slightly herby, matured whisky note comes through with a very thin glaze of a brittle toffee aroma. Rich and well made.

THE PALATE well matured and taut, with tannins, but it achieves a good balance with initially a rounded fruity note that then develops into full malty sweetness with some elements of both oak, toffee, and …

THE FINISH has a topping of oaky perfume notes that remind me of a 17-year-old Karuizawa. Then there is a good fudge note that is challenged by a little taut oak. That becomes a raw note like that of seed husks and it also acquires a little of a very faint note of both apples and some orange.

In spite of its name, this is not what we would normally call a malt whisky or single malt. Nikka All Malt is made from a blend of whiskies from the Miyagikyo and Yoichi distilleries. Each of these individually is admittedly made from just corn malt as the base material, but then distilled in a column still.

STRENGTH ETC. / SCORE: 1 2 3 4 5

NOSE: ....

PALATE: ....

FINISH: ....

NIKKA TAKETSURU, 12 YEARS OLD (40%)

I WOULD SAY THAT IT IS A NATIONAL CHARACTERISTIC for Japanese malt whisky to have a note of arrack. And this one is no different. It is a vatted malt that is supposed to have been blended from the medium-smoked Yoichi together with the fruitier Miyagikyo. The nose is like a thin slice of *Mettwurst* (German sausage) with a substantial dollop of fig jam—rich fruit and a faint burnt and slightly meaty aroma with spicy undertones as if the sausage had been rolled in pepper, rosemary, and thyme.

THE PALATE is at first medium bodied, chocolate-like, and slightly rugged. This is followed by a very well-balanced malt sweetness that rests on a faintly fiery note, a certain oaky ruggedness, and a delicious mixture of fruit and smoke again, but now more like bacon-wrapped oven-roasted dates. Very tasty.

THE FINISH is first a very good whisky taste, in which everything I look for in a 12-year-old well-matured whisky rolls in: raisins, oak, a little chocolate, a fairly unsweet malty note, and—after waiting a little while—there remains a balancing act between fruity sweetness and slightly fiery oak bitterness that is brilliant. Each well blended and well distilled in their different location. Quite simply great!

STRENGTH ETC. / SCORE: 1 2 3 4 5

NOSE: ....

PALATE: ....

FINISH: ....

NIKKA WHISKY

単一蒸溜所モルト

SINGLE MALT
"YOICHI"

余市

10
years old

余市蒸溜所10年貯蔵シングルモルト
Distilled & Matured in Yoichi Distillery The Nikka Whisky Distilling Co.,Ltd.
Product of Japan

NIKKA YOICHI, 10 YEARS OLD (45%)

ARRACK, SUNWARMED OAK, AND ACIDIC FRUIT—bitter oranges and overripe sweet oranges. A very light vanilla nose with a hint of a grassy, burnt note. Young spirit.

THE PALATE is sweet, balanced, and malty. The mouth-feel goes from smooth to fiery and with a continuing strong taste of malt. The body fills out more toward the end.

THE FINISH is pleasantly cask accented and malty. A faint bourbon-like note is there and it is met by a strong, dry maltiness that in a medium-long and vegetable dry, astringent finish ebbs into light vanilla and a surprising finale that becomes sweeter and sweeter and moves on toward fruit caramel with a little peat smoke.

My preference where Japanese whisky is concerned is for the bottlings that either maintain the chaser style or have a peaty, smoky note. Not that one excludes the other, but that these two elements are in my opinion the two that can become truly magnificent and rich with complexity. They are also particularly characteristic of Japanese whisky. In some cases the unique character of well-oak-matured, smoke-accented chaser is reinforced by the more incense-like Japanese oak making its own contribution.

STRENGTH ETC. / SCORE: 1 2 3 4 5

NOSE: ....

PALATE: ....

FINISH: ....

OCTOMORE 06.1 SCOTTISH BARLEY, 5 YEARS OLD (57%)

THE NOSE is smoky. Creamy salty notes are rounded off with a little sweetness. A faint, filling, and warm note of creamy gratinéed potatoes. The saltiness and acidity are reminiscent of anchovy-flavored, creamy Caesar salad dressing. It is soft, marine, and charming for those who like young smoky whisky. The aroma is high octane and warming, yet it is still impressively well integrated. Certainly some of us whisky drinkers' eyes glaze over when the phenols pile up as they do here, 167 p.p.m. to be precise. Funnily enough, adding water produces sweet, rounded aromas reminiscent of a several-decades-older Ardbeg whisky.

THE PALATE is surprisingly full bodied and has a tannin-like astringency. The fieriness increases. Ozone and salty and sweet licorice emerge until finally my mouth has watered so much that I must have diluted it to the strength of an unfortified wine. The palate is pleasant—young peaty whisky with a very promising body for a malt product that is merely five years old. Adding water produces a taste of hard unripe pears.

THE FINISH is initially a real salt attack. It has both ruggedness and a sweet note of tarred hemp rope. The saltiness lingers and is met by a rising grainy note. The heat lingers and the saltiness at times veers toward licorice root. The finish becomes smoother and shorter with water added.

A well-smoked recipe in stylish matt black packaging that promises much. For a spirit romantic like myself, almost perfect for a young smoky whisky, standing up well to the 6- to 7-year-old Ardbeg releases.

STRENGTH ETC. / SCORE: 1 2 3 4 5

NOSE: ....

PALATE: ....

FINISH: ....

OLD PULTENEY, 12 YEARS OLD (40%)

MILDLY FRUITY AND CHIRPY, with a teasingly amusing note of toffee sauce. There is a smoothness, like that of sweetly soft and malt syrup-drenched canned apricots. In the background there is also a slightly heavier, meatier note that provides an echo chamber for the sweetness, even though the hint of seaweed-spattered coastal whisky aroma that is there does not in any way conceal the view of the fruity sea breeze.

THE PALATE is initially smooth and sweet too. A very pleasant honey-sweet note comes in softly, arm in arm with a peppery warming alcohol note. This could be strong Polish mead for all I know. There is a fantastic and slightly oily full-bodied plumpness.

THE FINISH is a stage drier but it too has a big round honey note. There is more of the grain here than in the nose and the palate, and the initially full-bodied feel develops into a drier and gradually mildly rugged whisky note. I have said it before but I will say it again: this whisky is more than O.K. as it is, but with a café latte it is pure heaven. A whisky that makes an amateur Italian like myself roll his eyes, wave his arms about and exult— *molto molto bene*!

STRENGTH ETC. / SCORE: 1 2 3 4 5

NOSE: ....

PALATE: ....

FINISH: ....

177

OLD RIP VAN WINKLE, VAN WINKLE FAMILY RESERVE RYE, 13 YEARS OLD (47.8%)

DRY AND ASTRINGENT and yet with a scent of sweet fresh rye bread. There is a background aroma supporting the bread scent that is a compound mixture of fruit, perfume, a touch of varnish, and a hint of a flowery touch.

THE PALATE is initially sweet like cotton candy and rapidly becomes peppery on the tip of the tongue and severely taut in the mouth-feel. Here the oak comes into its own and is egged on by the rye in the base material, which also provides astringency in character. After a moment the sweetness and perfume in the mouth-feel increase.

THE FINISH is so dry that I find myself sitting and smacking my lips more than usual. There is a balance between a light perfumed fruity note and a dry rye and oak note. The lingering taste is mild, dry, fruity with a feeling that you have either eaten a chocolate praline filled with strawberry liqueur or that you have just downed a good rye. And you know which.

STRENGTH ETC. / SCORE: 1 2 3 4 5

NOSE: ....

PALATE: ....

FINISH: ....

PORT CHARLOTTE AN TURAS MOR (46%)

THE NOSE is lactic-acid-accented smoke with a rich, sweet note—a bit like the salty, slightly musty scent you notice if you stick your nose in a bag of oily, shiny, salty licorice. The nose is somehow typical of a full-bodied peaty whisky, but it has overtones of both peppermint and modeling clay.

THE PALATE is full bodied and fiery. Youthful heat on the tip of the tongue rests on a surprisingly full-bodied and robust malty sweetness. When the flames have died down the roasted walnut-like notes that cause this whisky to go up in people's estimation emerge.

THE FINISH is like salt licorice that yet retains some of the mouth-filling malty sweetness. The saltiness stays on the tongue and combines with the grainy element to produce an almost seaweed-like taste. To my mind an unusually successful young Islay whisky, with several surprising elements. One of the better ones so far from Bruichladdich, with the slightly smokier recipe called Port Charlotte on the bottle. The fact that the score is high is evident from the low level in the bottle if nothing else. I couldn't keep my greedy fingers away …

STRENGTH ETC. / SCORE: 1 2 3 4 5

NOSE: ....

PALATE: ....

FINISH: ....

181

POWERS GOLD LABEL (40%)

THIS WHISKEY HAS BEEN BLENDED since the 1960s, nowadays it is made at the Midleton Distillery. The nose has a fresh peppermint alcohol note with a noticeable strong spirit character. The nose is clean and well balanced, with very light notes of vanilla sweetness, a little fresh oak wood, and a little blackcurrant.

THE PALATE is first vanilla sweet, full and soft, fruity and round, so that it reminds me of the syrup that canned pears are in! Fiery alcohol catches up but is quite quickly tempered when the malty sweetness outweighs it, and it develops into a drier, bourbon cask-accented finale.

THE FINISH has an exuberant blend of light fieriness, clear sweetness, cask dryness, and a cotton-candy note, sweet but faintly burnt. In the longer perspective there is a mix of grain and sugar on the tongue, edged with an aroma of strong spirit.

If you want an alternative to the whiskey in your Irish coffee this one comes warmly recommended, a little more body, a little more character.

STRENGTH ETC. / SCORE: 1 2 3 4 5

NOSE: ....

PALATE: ....

FINISH: ....

183

REDBREAST IRISH SINGLE POT STILL, 12 VERSUS 15 YEARS OLD

Here is a comparison of two extraordinary pure pot-still whiskeys. Single pots only but not purely malted barley, hence this typical Irish whiskey type.

12 YEAR OLD (57.7%)

THE NOSE is strong and stickily fruity, prunes, mushy dried apricots, and a trace of ethyl acetate and oatcakes. With water the ultrasweet fruit aroma recedes. It develops into a balanced, drier aroma. Interesting scents of soft gingerbread and banana cake emerge and beneath them a faint meaty phenolic note, as sometimes found in a bitter ale. The palate is very fiery. With swilling comes a little honey, golden toast, and warm smooth oak. Well-baked puff pastry and something of rum and raisin chocolate. The finish is grassily astringent for a brief moment. It develops into vanilla notes that are met by fruit toffee aromas. The tannins make the tongue feel like fine sandpaper. With water the whole is subdued and the grain flavor comes through more clearly.

This single pot still was launched in 2012. In this case, quite apart from its considerable strength of just over 100 British Proof, it was batch number B1/11.

15 YEAR OLD (46%)

THE NOSE is faintly toffee-like with a hint of warm wood. It has notes of dill, a little dried fruit, and a little gasoline. There are notes of varnish and clear bourbon sweetness with toffee notes. Bordering that there is also something of damp wood. The palate is first a splash of pear. It is mild and faintly bitter from burnt sugar with a slightly flowery note. The finish is pure crème brûlée, with nutty notes of the toffee sweetness of almond cookies. This taste develops into butter toffee with a delicious burnt undertone. A likewise excellent single pot still, even though it must be said that the extra three years have heightened the complexity and chaser qualities a touch.

As you will already have suspected from the alcoholic strength, this whiskey is unfiltered.

RITTENHOUSE

STRAIGHT

Rye

WHISKY

Famous Straight Rye

40% Alc./Vol. (80 proof)

A rye whiskey distinguished for body and flavor.

Bottled by Continental Distilling Co., Bardstown, KY

RITTENHOUSE RYE (40%)

A GENEROUS AND FRUITY NOSE OF ROUNDED VANILLA with a hint of a sourish rye note. There is something of a dusty note, as in its many other American brethren. Honey, crystallized brown sugar, and cotton candy. Wet fresh oak wood. An edge of rye bread. Its strength, unusually low for an American whiskey—which is normally toward 45–50 percent— also helps to allow the sweetness and rounded vanilla notes have their say.

THE PALATE IS RUGGEDLY DRY and at the same time rounded with a certain sweetness. The mouth-feel is warmly fiery and just as genially sweet as the nose. The tautness increases toward the end. It is not sweetly ingratiating as a bourbon may often seem, but has more bite and a peppery, almost chili-sharp note.

THE FINISH IS TAUTLY RYE-BREAD ACCENTED. An unusually fine combination of bitterness and vanilla and a warmth from the spirit lingers briefly after I have swallowed a mouthful. My mouth is slightly numbed by the spirit even though the strength is relatively low. In the long finish there remains a candied sweet note and a mild vegetable bitterness. A very charming astringent rye whisky that goes excellently well with a decent-size piece of chocolate.

This producer is yet another of the many exceptions to the rule that Americans spell the word "whiskey." The full name is actually Rittenhouse Straight Rye Whisky.

STRENGTH ETC. / SCORE: 1 2 3 4 5

NOSE: ....

PALATE: ....

FINISH: ....

ESTD **ROYAL** 1845
LOCHNAGAR™
HIGHLAND SINGLE
MALT
SCOTCH WHISKY

LOCHNAGAR  DISTILLERY

DOUBLE MATURED
IN FINE OLD MUSCAT CASK-WOOD

Elegant and dry, in the Highland style, fine old Royal
Lochnagar invariably shows a pleasing citrus acidity and an
attractive, lingering finish. Skilled double maturation in old
Muscat cask-wood brings a sweet, floral richness to balance
this subtle sandalwood style and so reveals a deeper side of
this regal malt whisky.

DISTILLED 2000 BOTTLED 2012

BATCH NUMBER RL/00-12W

PRODUCED IN SCOTLAND BY
ROYAL LOCHNAGAR DISTILLERY
CRATHIE, BALLATER, ABERDEENSHIRE, AB35 5TB
S C O T L A N D

40%vol

ESTD **ROYAL** 1845
LOCHNAGAR™
HIGHLAND SINGLE
MALT
SCOTCH WHISKY

LOCHNAGAR DISTILLERY

THE
Distillers Edition™

DOUBLE MATURED IN FINE OLD MUSCAT CASK-WOOD
DISTILLED 2000 BOTTLED 2012

BATCH NUMBER RL/00-12W

40%vol PRODUCED IN SCOTLAND BY ROYAL LOCHNAGAR DISTILLERY,
CRATHIE, BALLATER, ABERDEENSHIRE, AB35 5TB, SCOTLAND

ROYAL LOCHNAGAR DISTILLERS EDITION RL/96-9T (40%)

THE NOSE is like sour dried figs with elements of fresh fruit and buttery brittle nuttiness like an almond-toffee chocolate bar. Nougat with cranberry influences, burnt sweet notes, and a hint of sweet licorice.

THE PALATE is extremely smooth and creamy. It could have been a sloppy meltdown of sweet fruit slush, but there is a fruit body of muscatel grapes, lychees, and cranberry sweetness with elements of milk chocolate—held in check by a backbone of spirit.

THE FINISH is as light footed as a cat on the tongue. It sweeps quickly past, leaving a very light peppery note with clear dry fruitiness.

Strangely enough, the berry-fruit character and faintly bitter finish greatly remind me of Japanese whiskies I have tried. There is nothing negative about this—on the contrary, this is one of the year's better whisky crosses for me.

It does not gain anything from adding water since it is smooth from the start; in fact it loses some of its rounded fruity character if it is watered down.

Matured in muscatel casks. Royal Lochnagar is a neighbor of Balmoral Castle. Queen Victoria is said to have rapidly become very fond of the distillery's expressive whisky. That is why she granted it the epithet "Royal" in its name.

STRENGTH ETC. / SCORE: 1 2 3 4 5

NOSE: ....

PALATE: ....

FINISH: ....

189

SHEEP DIP (40%)

STRAIGHTAWAY AN AROMA of almond paste and a distinct complex note of oak from a very carefully matured whisky. There is also an unusual and very fresh rustic scent of wet corn being mashed.

THE PALATE is at first from the cask, a little blackcurrant and a hint of a creamy note. It develops into a peppery heat and then turns into a more malty and honeysweet fullness. This fills out with a good fruity note, with some elements of both gooseberry and blackcurrant jam, together with a little strawberry preserve. This hovers between the heat and a base note of tannins. With this whisky flavor I take a fantastic aromatic holiday trip to Scotland with shortbread, Speyside whisky, and visits to distilleries!

THE FINISH is first honey, then malt with a little muffled note of peat that feels almost as if I had eaten smoked sausage about half an hour ago. This fades to quite a taut cask note and then there is a pure, light malty taste left in the mouth from this unusually successful malt blend.

It is said that "Sheep dip" is what the whisky-firing farmers chalked on the end of the cask when they stowed away their secret spirit—to make life harder for excise officers who perhaps gave the farmers cause to exclaim "deep shit" when the content of the cask was revealed. The Sheep Dip whisky sampled here has not been taxed either but is a private import. But its origin is noble, with the world-famous blender Richard Paterson as its creator. It is a blended malt from the Spencerfield Spirit Company and it consists of Scottish malt whisky that has been matured for between eight and sixteen years.

STRENGTH ETC. / SCORE: 1 2 3 4 5

NOSE: ....

PALATE: ....

FINISH: ....

191

ESTABLISHED 1828

CAMPBELTOWN SINGLE MALT SCOTCH WHISKY
PRODUCT OF SCOTLAND

SPRINGB
SPRING
SPRI
SPR

SPRINGBANK

AGED **10** YEARS
CAMPBELTOWN
SINGLE MALT

SPRINGBANK

DISTILLED & BOTTLED BY
J. & A. MITCHELL & CO.LTD. · CAMPBELTOWN · SCOTLAND

70cl   46%vol

PRODUCT O

NATUR

SPRINGBANK, 10 YEARS OLD (46%/57%)

A LIGHTLY BURNT, CARAMEL-SWEET, AND CEDARWOOD-LIKE NOSE of young whisky is what strikes you. A little nutty. Somewhat wet mustiness, albeit marginal. I think Springbank is at its best as a 15-year-old or more, but I have had to change my mind with this one. It is an amazingly good 10-year-old that even the nose shouts about. The stronger of the two 10-year-olds is of course sharp in the nose. It has only a little of the warm spicy woody character of the nose of the 46 percent variant, but after it has rested a moment in the glass a rich, sweet sherry note emerges from the alcohol.

THE PALATE is fiery and caramel filled, like a hearty butter toffee with chili spice in. Whether this is due to direct firing under the stills or not, the caramel sweetness of burnt sugar is palpable and absolutely positive. After swilling it a little in the mouth a faint peaty note comes through and blends into the sweetness and the roundedness. The taste of the 57 percent variant is fiery and chocolate-like with a slight raisiny edge without water. The finish is fiery and sticks to the tongue like crunchy caramel glue. The warmth lingers honorably and recedes and becomes slightly malty-sweet and peaty. As expected the intensity maintains a higher level than the 46 percent variant – and can of course be rationed as you wish!

THE FINISH OF THE WEAKER VARIANT is directly peaty and smoothes down to a balanced, sweet, yet well-adjusted, taut cask taste. A slightly woody burnt note with a peat smoke spine gradually looms out of the finish. An everyday whisky with class, and another really good 10-year-old.

STRENGTH ETC. / SCORE: 1 2 3 4 5

NOSE: ....

PALATE: ....

FINISH: ....

193

ESTABLISHED 1828

CAMPBELTOWN SINGLE MALT SCOTCH WHISKY
PRODUCT OF SCOTLAND

SPRINGBANK

AGED **15** YEARS

CAMPBELTOWN

SINGLE MALT

DISTILLED & BOTTLED BY J & CO LTD · CAMPBELTOWN · SCOTLAND

70cl

46%vol

SPRINGBANK, 15 YEARS OLD (46%)

HONEY AND FRUIT, a fresh, berry-like nose like cloudberry jam and fresh strawberry preserve in either nostril. A vigorous oak note that balances well on a wave of old chaser oakiness and light fresh wood.

THE PALATE is light and at the same time very rich. Freshly malty, fruity, and faintly sour. Full of life. Briefly I sense a beeswaxy honey-sweet note and toward the end even a mild phenolic scent of peat.

THE FINISH begins where the palate ends—sweet, berry-like, and flowery, with a fading peaty note. Mild toffee and faint phenolic smoke. A little popcorn? In all, such a complex, rich, and well-balanced whisky that perhaps some people might even find it overpolished. Whisky with built-in bling. There ought to be some on the shelf or in the mouth at home.

STRENGTH ETC. / SCORE: 1 2 3 4 5

NOSE: ....

PALATE: ....

FINISH: ....

SPRINGBANK, 18 YEARS OLD (46%)

LINGONBERRIES WITH MILK and a neighbor smoking cigarettes. Sourly berry-like and warming. Dry grey pears and a very faint peat smoke note.

THE IMMEDIATE MOUTH-FEEL is like balm, smooth and soft, full bodied. Sweetly fruity and balanced between cask and sweetness from both fruit and malt. Not a hint of heavy, cloying sweetness but a sprightly, acid-balanced sweetness that in spite of its age is not at all weighed down with wood, but simply balances like a line-dancing virtuoso.

IN THE FINISH first a short stab of cigarette smoke emerges and then it is filled out with fruit that has something of cherries, strawberries, dried prunes, and raisins—all in a compôte that you have in your hand without its being anything other than pleasant, thanks to a well-balanced tautness from the cask.

STRENGTH ETC. / SCORE: 1 2 3 4 5

NOSE: ....

PALATE: ....

FINISH: ....

197

- Tasmania Distillery -

SULLIVANS COVE

Rare

TASMANIAN

FRENCH OAK CASK MATURED

Single Cask Malt Whisky

HAND CRAFTED *to perfection*
...pot still, this Tasmanian
...LE MALT WHISKY
...distilled using renowned
...barley with only the

— DISTILLED WITH —
— CONVICTION —

PUREST WILDERNESS *...*
from local mountains and for...
Matured *in* HAND SELECT...
OAK *casks this single malt wh...*
offers an exotic taste experience

PRODUCT OF AUSTRALIA 700r...

SULLIVANS COVE FRENCH OAK PORT CASK (47.5%)

MY EXPECTATIONS were in my boots. Quite wrongly, but the last time I tried Tasmanian whisky there must have been something wrong with it. This one is good. The nose is generously exotic and fruity and tiptoes evenly between a well-smoothed and warmly spicy oak note.

THE PALATE is at first fiery and slowly develops into more of a Scotch-accented malty fruit. Fairly middle of the road to begin with, but even so not unfocused or heading for the ditch. Well made and quite rounded. The cask bitterness increases, taking over somewhat toward the end.

THE FINISH is at first astringent and fruity, somewhat like a slight grape seed flavor in its tannins. Considering the full, fruity astringency in the palate, the finish is surprisingly short, but with a good and lingering raisiny note. This remote distillery has succeeded extremely well with a delicious, barely 11-year-old malt for cold days in fall. But perhaps it also works well in warmer weather, with cheese. What do you think?

Tasmania Distillery was started in 1994 beside the Derwent River in Sullivans Cove, where Hobart was founded when the first British settlers arrived. The distillery changed hands in 2003 and moved to Cambridge, just outside Hobart. They now produce 120 casks containing 53 gallons (200 liters) of whisky at cask strength per year. In spite of its short history the distillery has won an impressive list of awards, amongst other things at the World Whisky Awards, and it also obtained 90–95 points in Jim Murray's Whisky Bible, together with favorable comments from the French wine critic Grégoire Sarafian.

STRENGTH ETC. / SCORE: 1 2 3 4 5

NOSE: ....

PALATE: ....

FINISH: ....

199

TALISKER, 10 YEARS OLD (45.8%)

A NOSE OF FRESH ALLSPICE with a clear spirit note and also quite a lot of sweetness.

THE PALATE is malty sweet and almost creamy to begin with. The maltiness becomes increasingly more honey flavored and fruity as it develops. Toward the end the seed notes dominate.

THE FINISH begins dry and with mildly sweet peat smoke. It goes on in a solid salty note reminiscent of salted peanuts and increases in sweetness somewhat. A long and balanced finish that also has a faint taste of white pepper. Brilliantly simple and with an original smoky character.

STRENGTH ETC. / SCORE: 1 2 3 4 5

NOSE: ....

PALATE: ....

FINISH: ....

201

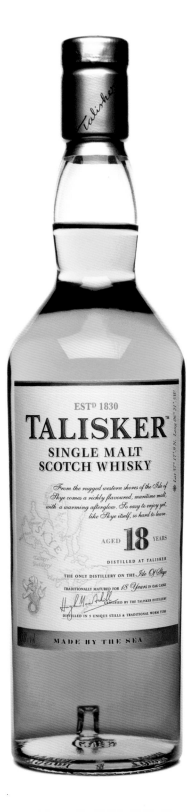

TALISKER, 18 YEARS OLD (45.8%)

STINGING SPIRIT NOSE with a faint whiff of wet dog. At the same time a compact, slightly dry-as-dust aroma of acidic dried fruit with a trace of vanilla. In the far distance there is a very, very faint whiff of smoke more reminiscent of an iron that has been left too long on a fine cotton shirt than of the peaty aroma of the 10-year-old.

THE PALATE is unappealing malty sweet, taut, and seed-husk-like, but with a growing sweetness. From the start there is the pepperiness typical of Talisker, and this increases and in the end acquires an increasingly clear peaty taste.

THE FINISH is caramel sweet and mild and clearly peat-smoky. The saltiness gradually increases and the initial taste is woven in to form more of a sweet cream sauce with a smoky bacon element.

One of my absolute favorites that in its quiet presence is more of a good friend to chat with than a party animal showering you with compliments and effusive garrulousness. A laidback whisky that is so moreish it is almost dangerous . . . .

STRENGTH ETC. / SCORE: 1 2 3 4 5

NOSE: ....

PALATE: ....

FINISH: ....

Talisker
ESTD 1830
TALISKER
SINGLE MALT
SCOTCH WHISKY
The Distillers Edition
DOUBLE MATURED IN AMOROSO CASK WOOD
DISTILLED 2001
BOTTLED IN 2012
TD-S: 50A
DISTILLED AT THE TALISKER DISTILLERY, CARBOST ISLE OF SKYE
FROM THE RUGGED WESTERN SHORES OF THE ISLE OF SKYE COMES A RICHLY FLAVOURED, MARITIME MALT
WITH A WARMING AFTERGLOW. SO EASY TO ENJOY YET, LIKE SKYE ITSELF, SO HARD TO LEAVE.
CERTIFIED BY THE TALISKER DISTILLERY
Lat 57° 17 '.9 N Long 6° 21 '.5W
DOUBLE MATURED IN
AMOROSO CASK WOOD FOR
A RICHER ROUNDED FLAVOUR
MADE BY THE SEA

TALISKER DISTILLERS EDITION (45.8%)

A FAINT BALANCED APPLE-PEAT TONE with a slight sour dish-towel note that is almost concealed by a spirituous nose with a tinge of fresh mint.

THE PALATE IS VERY SMOOTH and malty with a caramel-sweet roundedness that almost conceals the smokiness. The spirit makes itself felt and with it more of the peat, even though a malty, berry-like sweetness still dominates.

THE FINISH BEGINS PEPPERY and raisin sweet with clearer smoky phenols. It develops into a sherry-cask and white pepper taste. The finale is very pleasing in this instance—the taste is a quiet balance between sherry-matured whisky and faint phenols. A moment later there is a hint of a nutmeg feel that yet retains a faint peaty note. This whisky hits the jackpot with its balance, although I could well have envisaged a slightly bolder presentation of its obvious qualities.

Matured in the sweetened version of oloroso sherry that is called amoroso. We might also mention that the odd number on Talisker's alcohol content has to do with the British standard. To compare the incompatible units 80 British Proof has been converted to the almost exactly correct 45.8 percent. Otherwise 70 British Proof corresponds to 40 percent ABV and 75 corresponds to 43. You see the pattern? This explains a few things about the labels, don't you think?

STRENGTH ETC. / SCORE: 1 2 3 4 5

NOSE: ....

PALATE: ....

FINISH: ....

TEELING WHISKEY–RUM CASK (46%)

A DELICIOUS NOTE of caramelized sugar is the first thing that strikes me. Faint vanilla and fudge emerge in the continuation and a very light note of fresh blackcurrants combines in a warm, embracing mixture of soft wood aromas and a sourish fresh oak note, rounded off with a little ripe banana and almonds.

THE PALATE is at first smooth and a certain fieriness expands. The cask character is delicate and tends more toward bourbon cask, no—actual bourbon! With a little time a rum taste with full-bodied ripe fruit and faint arrack emerges, and in spite of this it maintains a balance with a stable dry base, thanks to the tannins of the oak.

THE FINISH has a light white pepper note and tends toward more of both seed husks and a rugged oak character. A strange, but not uneven note remains that reminds me of mushrooms. Amusingly enough, this is something I often notice in Bacardi rum. Perhaps some misgiving about the choice of cask. It was delicious anyway!

This welcome newcomer has the same name as Cooley's founder. His sons Jack and Stephen Teeling run the business, and the sharp-eyed may spot a chimney of the father's estate, Kilbeggan, in the distance. Cooley's in itself is no longer in the family since it was sold to Jim Beam in 2011 for 71 million Euros, something that Stephen quoted as the reason for leaving Cooley's to devote himself to marketing in the new family firm instead.

(Source The Spirits Business, 5 June 2013)

STRENGTH ETC. / SCORE: 1 2 3 4 5

NOSE: ....

PALATE: ....

FINISH: ....

TEERENPELI KASKI (43%)

YOUNG FRESH OAK, malty, brisk sweetness, and a caramel note with a faint whiff of sulfur that has elements of both pretzels and a little gunpowder.

THE PALATE is fiery and spry, young and sherry accented. There are marmalade-like fruit notes that hover in a vigorous, hot-tempered fieriness.

THE FINISH has a little of marzipan and almond, together with a berry-like, faint sulfurus note that also has clear elements of sherry and a touch of peaty phenols.

This represents a big step forward for Finnish whisky. Some people might perhaps turn their noses up at the sulfur note, but I don't. I think it maintains a decent standard and a standard that comes together perfectly with the fruitiness from the sherry cask maturation, so that it does not finish up with the whole tongue stuck in the marmalade jar.

STRENGTH ETC. / SCORE: 1 2 3 4 5

NOSE: ....

PALATE: ....

FINISH: ....

209

THOMAS H. HANDY SAZERAC RYE (66.35%)

STRAIGHT FROM THE CASK and without water this premium American is an absolute bombshell in nose and palate. The nose is very concentrated and has clear traits of sour rye, and this in a compact, dark, molasses bread tone. The note of a crispy caramel sugar that is usually found in a good American whiskey of some age is present here too, but cooked down to a wall of toffee, strangely enough with an overtone of floweriness and an almost rose-like aroma.

THE PALATE is a concentrate of whiskey aroma. It has oak cask-aging traits and likewise an intense flavor of both the base material, the astringently sour rye. and the burnt, sugared, spirit-soaked oak cask that the whiskey has been kept in. There is a note of marinated dried fruit that has more of a burnt bittersweet tone than the ingratiating smoothness of the sugar sweetness.

THE FINISH is first very cask bitter, but gradually develops into a wood-enhanced tautness that nevertheless has a layer of sweetness, like sweet fig jam and dried prunes. A dry mineral note lingers and finally there is also a little earthy and flowery aroma that almost reminds you of wet compost.

STRENGTH ETC. / SCORE: 1 2 3 4 5

NOSE: ....

PALATE: ....

FINISH: ....

211

W.L. WELLER, 12 YEARS OLD (45%)

A LIGHT NOSE with notes of ripe honeydew melon and a little fudge with a barely perceptible cream note. There is also a note of the oak cask that is roasted wood with an elegant lightness, a faint pepperiness, and something that in terms of scent lies between grass and parsley.

THE PALATE is initially very smooth. The fieriness increases and also a ruggedness from the oak that makes the twelve years felt. The whole develops into an intricate mixture of varnish, an ingratiating fruit flavor, and also a sweetness with a touch of floweriness, pulled together with oak bitterness and a mineral-accented dryness.

THE FINISH is at first grassily bitter and wanders on vanilla-sprinkled paths toward a longer finale where the taste is more of cream and jelly beans. It feels very well made and the venerable age's austere attributes are nicely met with a complex sweetness that has elements both of ripe fruit and fiery alcohol and of cask-like toffee notes.

W.L. Weller is made by the Buffalo Trace Distillery in Frankfort in Kentucky. Old William LaRue Weller (1825–99), who gave the whiskey its name, claimed to have been the first in Kentucky to make a bourbon in which all the rye was replaced with wheat. It is claimed that this was made and sold for the first time in 1849, and even today it says "Wheated bourbon" on the label on the bottle.

STRENGTH ETC. / SCORE: 1 2 3 4 5

NOSE: ....

PALATE: ....

FINISH: ....

213

WHISKY GLOSSARY

ABV: Alcohol by volume. Put simply, the alcohol content as a percentage of the volume as it is normally measured now.

ALAMBIC: The name given to pot-still-type stills in France. The Cognac district has given its name to the type of still used there, namely *Alambic charentais*.

ALDEHYDES: A group of chemical substances that, expressed simply, are alcohols that have lost one hydrogen atom. In one form an aldehyde called acetaldehyde is formed when ethanol is exposed to air for a lengthy period. It is often aldehydes people are referring to when they say the whisky smells of various flowers. Other familiar smells with aldehydes as a base are those of nutmeg and cinnamon (*cinnamaldehyde*), vanilla (*vanillin*), and bitter almond (*benzaldehyde*)—as in amaretti or Italian cookies!—and also the scent of cloves associated with the casks (*eugenol*).

AMYLASE: A group of enzymes that break down starch. As far as whisky is concerned they are in the mashing, where they are present in the barley and break down the starch into fermentable types of sugar.

ANGEL'S SHARE: That part of the maturing whisky that evaporates from the casks. So-called because it is this free ration that the angels are supposed to party with. Happily it is tax-free, but it represents a devastating loss—some 2–3 percent per annum of all the whisky that is matured in Scotland, and more like 5–6 percent of the whisky maturing in Kentucky!

ANOSMIA: Full or partial absence of the sense of smell. This can be caused by accidents such as a hard knock to the head and it may also be inborn.

ARRACK: Originally distilled from sugar-cane juice amongst other things. The distillate has a typical aroma that can often be smelled in spirits that have been matured for a long time. In Scandinavia arrack is an ingredient in punch and the chocolate-tipped green marzipan rolls served with coffee, amongst other things. The arrack aroma in matured spirits is directly related to fusel oil and is often found in matured fruity spirits that, after distillation, contain a high level of the heavier alcohols. The aroma is sometimes found in whisky, even more frequently in cognac, and above all in dark rum.

BARLEY: The grain whose mere existence and happy composition has proved extraordinarily good for manufacturing alcoholic grain-based drinks. A high starch content and plenty of enzymes that can break down the starch into fermentable sugar. The commonest varieties are two-row and six-row barley, of which the two-row is used in making whisky.

BARRELS: Casks in general but also more specifically whiskey casks from the USA, where they hold about 48 gallons (180 liters).

BLENDED WHISKY: Whisky blended from strong spirits, grain whisky, and single malt whisky. Typical proportions are 30 percent malt whisky from about twenty kinds and the remainder grain whisky.

BPS: British Plain Spirit, rough spirit from the still. The term is often used to explain what is meant in statistics when writing about volumes produced.

BUTT: The name of a size of cask, about 132 gallons (500 liters), but it varies, depending on who is counting and on what basis, from 130 gallons (491 liters) up to 168 gallons (636 liters). Originally a type of sherry cask.

COLUMN STILL, CONTINUOUS STILL, PATENT STILL: a still also known as a Coffey still after its inventor, the Irish excise officer Aeneas Coffey.

CUT: The extent to which the rough spirit is taken out, determined by what character the maker wants from the distillate in the last still. A broad cut ensures that both lighter and heavier substances are taken before and after the ethanol, while a narrow cut means that a scant part of the heart of the distillation is taken in order to maintain a purer and more neutral spirit.

DEXTRIN: Unfermentable type of sugar that occurs when starch is broken down by high heat. Think of the browning on muffins. It is dextrin that has been created in the heat of the oven.

DIASTASE: One of the enzymes that helps to break up starch into fermentable types of sugar, for example malt sugar.

DRAFF: The residues of the malt that are left when the brewer's wort has been strained off. Left in the bottom of the mashing vat and used as animal feed.

DREGS: Generally sludgy residues, particularly the fine mud that collects at the bottom of the mashing vat, in a still column, or in the bottom of a cask.

ESTERS: A group of chemical compounds that are formed when an acid reacts with an alcohol and with a surplus of water forms a scented ester. Another type of ester is wax that is formed if a fatty acid with a long carbon chain reacts with an alcohol. If the alcohol is a glycerol the result also becomes a fat. Esters may have, amongst other things, fruity scents, and they may also be used as solvents. Typical scents for esters are apple (the ester *amyl butyrate*), pear (*amyl acetate*), rose (*geraniol*), and *ethyl acetate*—mentioned several times in the book as the scent of glue and nail varnish.

ETHEREAL: Means the airy scent of volatile substances, chiefly light, fresh, perfume-like scents from the plant kingdom. The origin of the word is volatile oils from plants, so-called ethereal (essential) oils.

EUGENOL: Pronounced *ew-gee-nol*. This is the aromatic substance found in cloves. An aromatic alcohol that is strongly bactericidal. It has been used amongst other things in dentistry as a disinfectant. That is why it is a scent that many older people associate with less than happy memories. In whisky the scent can be derived from substances that may originate from the oak wood and also the rough spirit.

FEINTS: English for the tails or final spirit of the distillation, in other words that part of the distillation that goes for redistilling because it contains too many of the heavier alcohols.

FIRST-FILL CASK: A term relating to when the rough whisky is placed in casks that are being filled for the first time with whisky after having previously contained, for example, bourbon or sherry.

FUSEL OIL: The collective name for heavier alcohols that are processed in a teasing and stepmotherly fashion. This is in spite of the fact that together with their younger siblings in the heads of the distillation they are one of the prerequisites for an eventful and aroma-promoting maturation.

GERANIOL: The aromatic that gives the rose geranium (*Pelargonium graveolens*) for instance its typical sharp, fresh, invigorating, almost peppermint-like scent.

GRAIN WHISKY: A whisky made in a column still with higher purity and fewer flavor-giving substances.

GREEN MALT: Barley that has been softened by steeping in water. Through the kilning, the roasting of the green malt, green malt loses its prefix—it becomes just malt.

HEADS: The first part of three stages in the final distillation. Rises as steam through the neck of the still at the start of the distillation, in other words in the heating up. The heads therefore contain lighter substances such as flower- and fruit-scented aldehydes and esters, and also methanol. Like fusel oil it is to some extent a desirable substance to give the whisky potential for development during maturation.

HEART/CUT: The central part of the second distillation. *Coeur* in French. Usually taken out at a strength of between 72 and 73 percent and down to 59–68 percent alcohol.

HIGHLANDS: According to a tax law of 1784 the area north of a line running roughly between Perth and Glasgow. Like the Lowlands, it is a historic regional division of Scotland that is associated with whisky. The Highlands have distilleries with small stills that often produce whisky that is flavorsome, malty sweet, mild, and full-bodied.

HOGSHEAD: Name of a size of cask, usually 66 gallons (250 liters), but in exceptional cases it can be up to 73 gallons (275 liters).

ISLANDS: The collective term that the whisky industry has given the collection of islands round Scotland that make a more or less similar whisky, usually with the exception of Islay, which has to stand alone. The group includes Highland Park and Scapa on Orkney, Tobermory/Ledaig on Mull, Isle of Jura, and Talisker on Skye. Characteristic for these, to varying degrees, are the marine character, iodine, the sea, tar, and in some cases peppery "caskiness" and a salt-drenched sea breeze.

ISLAY: This well-known island in the Atlantic houses eight distilleries and about 3,500 people, plus an unknown number of sheep and tourists. The first destination on a trip from the southern end of the island is the place known as Port Ellen, where the distillery of the same name closed down in 1983. The warehouses can be seen when you arrive at the harbor on the ferry. In terms of whisky only the Port Ellen Maltings are active today, as one of Scotland's smallest industrial maltings. Then away to the east along a country road lie Ardbeg, Lagavulin, and Laphroaig. A step further up to Port Askaig and you have Bunnahabhain and Caol Ila, then onward toward the west to the place and the distillery called Bowmore, across the creek to Bruichladdich, and out along the western side to the little, newly started Kilchoman. The last is one of the three or four most recently started distilleries and is now the westernmost in Scotland.

KETONES: Chemical compounds that produce several of the more far-out aromas of whisky. Amongst other things the substance that produces a cheese-like scent, diacetyl, belongs to this group of compounds. Other aromas that have ketones as their source are raspberries (*ionone*), violets, and both hay and new-mown grass.

KILN: The building where the germinating green malt is roasted to stop it sprouting. In principle the building is a fireplace with a fine mesh grid floor where heat and often peat smoke as well seep up through the green malt, producing roasting and sometimes flavor. The kiln often has the characteristic pagoda-like roof that is typical of whisky distilleries.

LOMOND STILL: A hybrid of a column still and a pot still. Constructed with the idea of being able to produce different types of rough spirit by varying the degree of distillation in one and the same still.

LOWLANDS: Under a tax law of 1784 southern Scotland, below a designated line running roughly between Perth and Glasgow. The regional division of Scotland that, like the Highlands, in terms of whisky has a clear historical background. With its large stills and triple distillation, the Lowlands often produce a whisky that is light and also fruity.

LYNE ARM: The narrowed opening of copper pot stills that malt whisky is distilled in, resembling a swan's neck.

MASHING: The processing stage in which warm water causes the barley enzymes to break down the starch into fermentable sugar.

OAK: Type of wood that in some cases is very well suited for making casks for storing drink. There are about six hundred kinds of oak, of which only a handful are suitable for the manufacture of drink casks. The oak imparts tannins to the drink and thus balances the drink's sweetness and tautens, strengthens, and completes the properties of the cask contents. The commonest species for maturing whisky are the European sessile oak *Quercus petraea* and the common oak *Quercus robur*. In the USA the white oak or *Quercus alba*, which provides less flavor and color, dominates. It has a less complex flavor, paler color, and more evident taut woody character coupled with distinct vanilla. The Japanese *Quercus mongolica*, mizunara, or Mongolian oak is sporadically used in Japan and produces a more incense-accented, warm woody note with elements of sandalwood, cedar, and aloe wood.

PEAT: Turf, in other words incompletely decayed plant elements that, when they are burned, produce a varying character in the peat smoke, depending on what types of plant the peat has originated from.

PERTHSHIRE: The central part of the southern Highlands that houses a couple of distilleries. May be said to be typical of the Highlands as a whole.

PINT: Well-known measure of beer that more precisely is 0.5678 liters, or 20 fluid ounces, or 2 cups!

PIPE: The name of a cask size, usually around 132 gallons (500 liters) and originating as a storage cask for port wine, often referred to as a *port pipe*.

POT ALE: The remains of the wash after distillation, also called burnt ale.

POT STILL: The enclosed pot that ensures that a steaming, boiling wash or weak spirit can be distilled to a stronger alcoholic liquid.

REFLUX: Flowback, referring to how much of what is condensed inside the whisky still runs back and therefore has a chance to be distilled again during boiling. The higher the reflux, the lighter and purer the rough spirit.

RUMMAGER: An arrangement of chain-bearing arms that spin round slowly inside directly fired whisky pots to ensure that the liquid does not burn on the bottom of the pan.

SLÀINTE: "Cheers" in Gaelic. Pronounced roughly "slant-dje." Often heard incorporated loudly and slurred in many other languages. "To your good health," or "Skål" according to Swedish tradition, is more precisely "Slàinte mhòr agad!" which is to be pronounced "slant-dje voor agg-erd!" You often see the somewhat simpler form "Slàinte math!" which translates as "Good health!" in which the second part is pronounced roughly as "và!"

SPENT LEES: The bottom dregs in the distillation pot.

SPIRIT SAFE: The aquarium-like, generally well-polished, brass and glass box that allows closed handling of the cut. Introduced from the start in conjunction with the changes to the law brought in in 1823. Tested for the first time at the Port Ellen distillery and invented by a Mr. Septimus Fox.

STEEPING: The first step in malting, when the barley is thoroughly wetted. It is normally steeped three times and drained so that soon after that it will begin to germinate.

TAILS: That part of the final distillation that occurs when the heat has increased in the still to the degree that heavier substances rise up through the swan's neck for subsequent condensation. This includes for instance what we call fusel oil.

TANNIN: The same thing as tannic acid. This is found in relatively plentiful quantities in oak, which benefits the content of the cask in both rioja wines and malt whisky. Also found for example in fir trees, which is where the acids got their name since fir bark was historically used in the tanning of leather.

TERPENES: This group of naturally occurring chemical compounds includes aromatic substances, usually from trees, composed of isoprene units. Terpenes produce scents of crude rubber, caraway (*carvone*), menthol, mint, and camphor (*camphane*).

TOFFEE SAUCE: In order to achieve the toffee note typical of many types of whisky, the following is recommended. Place a saucepan on the hob over medium heat, spoon in about 2 ounces (50 g) of butter, melt it and add about half a cup (100 ml) of light cream and possibly more later if you think the consistency requires it. Then stir in 2 tablespoons of molasses syrup, 2 tablespoons of superfine sugar, and a pinch of salt. Stir the mixture together and leave to simmer over low heat for 15–20 minutes until when you drop a little of the sauce into cold water it begins to set. If you have a thermometer it should show 248 °F (120 °C). Serve trickled over vanilla ice cream, a few slices of banana, and crushed amaretti, and drink a little bourbon or a Glenlivet Nadurra with it. Enjoy a blessed marriage!

UISGE BEATHA: Scottish Gaelic for "water of life." Note that the word for whisky has come from the anglicization of the Gaelic for water.

VANILLIN: An aldehyde with a scent that is one of those that the human sense of smell finds it easiest to sense in small concentrations. Vanillin comes partly from the eugenol in the rough whisky and partly from the oak. From oak the vanillin is a result of the breaking down of the sizing agent, lignin, in oak wood that occurs when the inside of the cask is roasted or burnt. In chemical terms vanillin is an aldehyde, closely related to aromatics found in nutmeg and cloves.

VATTED WHISKY: Whisky blended from different single malts. Now also called blended malt. Comes from vat, meaning cask.

WASH STILL: Also called a low-wine still owing to what runs off from the still. This is the name of the first still of the two that the Scots distill in as a rule.

WASH: Wort that has been given an addition of yeast until it has finished fermenting and is to be distilled. Usually has an alcohol content of 7–9 percent, but varies, depending on the manufacturer, between 4 and 11 percent.

WOOD FINISH: Finishing maturation by changing casks to some that are slightly sweeter, fruitier, or simply more strongly flavored. Found for instance in Glenmorangie that has used Sauternes, port, and sherry maturation, or Balvenie that has both more pronounced sherry and bourbon maturations and also a smooth port wine finish. As a rule the finishing takes place in first-time casks and lasts between six months and a couple of years. If it is done well it balances against the whisky character that should be apparent in the interaction with the glaze of the final maturation found on top of a good basic maturation.

WORT: The sugar solution containing chiefly water and malt sugar that is the result of mashing.

YEAST: Unicellular fungus whose effect on sugar is—gratifyingly—carbon dioxide and ethanol. Its magical effect was hidden until the middle of the nineteenth century when, amongst others, Emil Christian Hansen of Carlsberg discovered in 1883 that the fantastic magic was the consequence of a controllable fungus that could be cultivated and developed in the required direction.

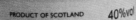

DALLAS DHU

BOTTLED 2010

70cl   PRODUCT OF SCOTLAND   40%vol

SPEYSIDE

SINGLE MALT
SCOTCH WHISKY

DISTILLED **1982** DISTILLED

BOTTLED BY
GORDON & MACPHAIL
ELGIN·SCOTLAND

THANKS TO

FIRST AND FOREMOST, THANK YOU TO ...
My dear and loving family: **PIA, KLARA, LIINA,** and **JULIA.**

AND OF COURSE A BIG THANK YOU ALSO TO ...
GRENADINE and **STEVALI**, and especially **ALAN MARANIK**, for their supportive and patient work on the original work, ideas, and marketing, and also to speedy **BENNY ERONSON** for the proofreading. Likewise warm thanks for all their help with the pictures and so on go to the following:

HELENA EDBLADH (Casksweden)

ISABELLE HAMILTON, JOSEFINE ELIDIUS, RICHARD VIITANEN (Edrington Sweden)

ANGELA FRIBERG

CHRISTINE J. MCCAFFERTY AND JOANNE MCKERCHAR (Diageo)

CAROLINE LÅFTMAN (Philipson & Söderberg)

JONAS OLSSON (Nigab)

HELÉNE REUTERWALL-THIDEMAN (Pernod Ricard)

… and finally all of you who have contributed generously to earlier vintages of this book!

Copyright © Örjan Westerlund and Stevali Production
Original title: *101 whisky du måste dricka innan du dör 2014/2015*

ISBN of the original edition: 978-91-86287-42-9

Photography: Örjan Westerlund, apart from
Cask Sweden, page 88.
Diageo, pages 58–60, 116, 128, 140, 188, 200–204 (images courtesy of the Diageo Archive).
Edrington Sweden, pages 26, 66, 102–108, 124, 130–136, 144–154, 160.
Mackmyra Whisky, page 156.
Möet Hennessy, pages 18–24, 92, 98.
Pernod Ricard, pages 90, 142, 182.
Philipson & Söderberg, page 74.
William Grant & Sons/Nigab, pages 34–36, 80–84.

Product idea and Creative Director: Stefan Lindström
Graphic design and production: Alan Maranik/Stevali Production
Text editing: Jennifer Lindström and Benny Eronson

© of the English edition: h.f.ullmann publishing GmbH
Special edition
Translation from Swedish: Julie Martin in association with
First Edition Translations Ltd, Cambridge, UK
Editing and typesetting: First Edition Translations Ltd, Cambridge, UK
Project management: Isabel Weiler, Katharina Pferdmenges
Overall responsibility for production: h.f.ullmann publishing GmbH, Potsdam, Germany

Printed in China, 2014
ISBN 978-3-8480-0687-8
10 9 8 7 6 5 4 3 2 1
X IX VIII VII VI V IV III II I

www.ullmann-publishing.com
newsletter@ullmann-publishing.com
facebook.com/ullmann.social